808.80354
Treasury of wedding poems,
quotations, and short
c1998.

/01

Treasury of

Wedding

Poems, Quotations, and Short Stories

Compiled by the Editors of
Hippocrene Books

Illustrated by
Rosemary Fox

Treasury of

Wedding

Poems, Quotations, and
Short Stories

Compiled by the Editors of
Hippocrene Books

Illustrated by
Rosemary Fox

Hippocrene Books, Inc.
New York

For information, address:
HIPPOCRENE BOOKS, INC.
171 Madison Avenue
New York, NY 10016

ISBN 0-7818-0636-4

Library of Congress Cataloging-in-Publication Data available

Printed in the United States of America.

✦⁕ Contents ⁕✦

❖ Quotations ❖ 57

❖ Short Stories ❖ 85

❖ Selected Biographies ❖ 133

Poems

Proposal

BAYARD TAYLOR

The violet loves a sunny bank,
The cowslip loves the lea,
The scarlet creeper loves the elm,
But I love—thee.

The sunshine kisses mount and vale,
The stars they kiss the sea,
The west winds kiss the clover bloom,
But I kiss—thee.

The oriole weds his mottled mate,
The lily's bride o' the bee;
Heaven's marriage ring is round the earth,—
Shall I wed thee?

from **The Bells**

EDGAR ALLAN POE

Hear the mellow wedding bells—
Golden bells!
What a world of happiness their harmony foretells!
Through the balmy air of night
How they ring out their delight!—
From the molten-golden notes,
And all in tune,
What a liquid ditty floats
To the turtle-dove that listens, while she gloats
On the moon!
Oh, from out the sounding cells,
What a gush of euphony voluminously wells!
How it swells!
How it dwells
On the Future!—how it tells
Of the rapture that impels
To the swinging and the ringing
Of the bells, bells, bells,—
Of the bells, bells, bells,
To the rhyming and the chiming of the bells!

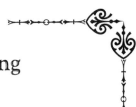

Village for a Wedding

Jan Boleslaw Ozog

Sky like the pigeon's little belly.

Sky like a goldfinch egg,
sky like a starling's tune,
greenish blue.

But fields like the sun-drenched sea
where deer bound through oats
like fish through a sea of rye.

And the distant village from a hammock
like a chain on a bicycle.

Iris in golden sheen like a pilot flame.

But trees deep-rooted like ponds
of green broth.
But grass like prayers
from lips of decaying willows.

And the distant village from a hammock
harrows, gouged by nails
instead of stakes.

Ladybugs slide off lindens,
roaches to pick in a handkerchief.

In barns peasant gears groan,
cranking round the chaff-cutter,
and frightened wasps play
like a heathen church at high mass.

Red beaks of carrots circle higher than storks.

And the power station beyond the village
limping on crutches like bent herdsmen on a crook.

Here the hemp-scented morning
salted with a bundle of clover;

Here my beloved hides for the night
safe from the boys in the kneading trough.
Up the ladder to the attic
carrying a measure of rye on his back
like a good husband—

Here you are invited to the wedding.

This and More

GLENN SIEBERT

Attenders to this day:
Look, the wedding is a reason
To inspect your thoughts; say
Smily wishes to the young wedded,
But see to your own new season—
No trite impediments, no bored white
Winter of cold thoughts imbedded
In mountain crevices of self-pity.
Be gathered into the light,
Into no mere festivity—
But more, a snowballing of hope.
Then you still live; we all
Live on tomorrow when two breaths elope,
Tonight when pulse on pulse sustains
Two lives, these and their sweet flesh...
Inhale brisk flowers, then let befall
Whatever dark rains
Come; you see lives mesh
Today, today you bystand bliss.
Attend all this.

POEMS

from The Bait

JOHN DONNE

Come live
with me, and be my love,
And we will
some new pleasures prove,
Of golden sands,
and crystal brooks,
With silken lines,
and silver hooks.

Bride

George Sarandáris

Joy comes to us as a bride
The first rains burst into bloom
Nightingales strike up a dance in our neighborhood
Elegant water nymphs bring songs
Thoughts turn into gold
And gold all conversation
Poets and girls
Learn kisses by heart
Someone arrives at the festival out of breath
It is Time with his flute

Bride's Mother

CHRISTIE LUND

They see you as a woman, as a bride,
    Sweet in a modeled gown of creamy lace;
Your blue eyes turned to him in trust and pride,
    Your golden curls a halo for your face.
Yet I, your mother, see you not as this
    Alone: I see you as a baby in my arms,
Helpless and small, mine to adore and kiss;
    I see you as a child of three whose charms
And childish laughter are for me alone;
    I see your first, brief step beside my knee;
I see you in the years when you have grown
    Into the lovely woman that they see.
A thousand priceless memories I keep
    Within my heart. Forgive me that I weep.

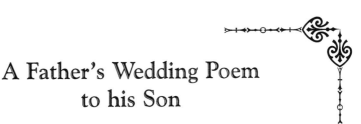

A Father's Wedding Poem
to his Son

JOSEPH EZOBI

My son, on this thy wedding day rejoice,
To song of mirth attune thy heart and voice.
Take thou the graceful doe, the royal bride,
With her thy joy and happiness divide.
A comely form, my darling son, is thine;
Corrupt it not, for 'tis a gift divine.
If thou wouldst see the gates of Paradise,
Refrain! Thy work on earth will thee suffice.
Yea, many rushing heaven's height to scale
In fruitless quests their life misspent bewail.
Behold reveal'd creation's mystery,
List to the strains of heaven's symphony;
And when the day of good report is nigh
E'en as Elijah thou shalt rise on high.
Three crowns there are, and these the world may love;
A blameless name is more, all crowns above.
Humbly pray God may crown thee with His Light,
To live 'mid men, with heart, with soul, with might.
Rejoice with her, thy graceful tender dove;
God bless you twain, with love as angels love.

translated by D. I. Freedman

Wedding Season

J. L. RUNEBERG

The daughter said to her aged mother:
"May I not this fall my wedding keep?"
The mother answered: "Let it be till spring;
Spring, O daughter, is best for wedding suited,
even birds build their nests in spring."
The daughter said: "Why wait til spring,
why is spring for wedding best suited,
what of it, if birds in spring their nests do build?
Each season, my good mother, is best suited
for the one who loves each season."

translated by Börje Vähämäki

Marriage Vow

UNKNOWN CHINESE POET, HAN DYNASTY

(206 B.C.–A.D. 221)

O, celestial beings
Let our feelings for each other
Continue without diminishing
Only when mountains are leveled
To basins, when ocean waters run
Dry, when winter is ripped
With thunders, when the summer sky
Rains snow, and heaven and earth
Are smashed together, shall we
Ever dare to be parted.

With This Ring I Thee Charm

Saul Tchernikhovsky

With this ring I thee charm in the rite
Of the butterfly born to its world,
To its life of one day, the bridal night
Of one hour amid colored wings.
With this ring I thee charm in the plight
Of choirs of mosquitoes that dance
In the forest clearing, in the light
Of their mute song of noon's fiery romance.

With this ring I thee charm in the rite
Of the rustling tree and the plants
Fluttering in the breeze, that recite
In the tongue of aromas and speak only scents.
With this ring I thee charm in the ways
Of that great yearning that sings,
The great yearning, so silent always,
That blossoms again every year, every spring.

With this ring I thee charm in the rite
Of the bellowing deer that broods,
In longing for a mate, at twilight,
With glowing horns at the edge of the woods.
With this ring I thee charm with the power
Of all the might in animal essence,
Of worlds once destroyed and reborn in the roar
Of all the thousands of tribes of existence.

With this ring I thee charm, in the deep
Secret of all the poems of man and his song,
Of his magician's words, of the glories that sleep
In the mysteries of his faith, hidden so long
In the guess and the stress of each human heart,
In the source of his dance and the base of his art.
Bewitched, now be still—and never depart—
I thee charm forever... till death do us part...

The Wedding Gift

MINNA IRVING

In the garret under the sloping eaves
    Stood Grandmother Granger's old hair trunk,
With battered bureaus and broken chairs,
    And a spinning wheel and similar junk.
The hirsute cover was worn in spots;
    'Twas once the hide of a bridle cow,
That grazed of yore in the meadows green
    Where Harlem flats are towering now.

I used to climb the garret stairs
    On a rainy day and lift the lid
And loose the fragrance of olden times
    That under the faded finery hid—
Damask roses and lavender,
    Delicate odors, fine and faint,
Clinging still to the crumpled folds
    Of silks and muslin and challies quaint.

Fans and slippers and veils were there,
    Beads of amber and yellow lace,
Coral earrings and Paisley shawls,
    And the big pink bonnet that framed her face
With its golden curls and soft blue eyes,
    And the dimpled chin and the laughing lip,
When Grandfather Granger took his bride
    And the smart new trunk on a wedding trip.

It was the soul of a garden old,
    Dreaming under the stars, I freed.
Jasmine, lilies, and rosemary,
    Stately marigolds gone to seed.

Thyme and pansy and mignonette,
　　Sage and balsam and love-in-a-mist,
Where Grandfather Granger, a bold young blade,
　　Scaled the walls to the secret tryst.

To the creak and sway of a four-horse stage
　　He kissed her hand in its silken mitt,
And her girlish cheek that was like a rose
　　As her blissful blushes mantled it.
The honeymoon never waned, they say—
　　The pair were lovers through all the years,
Gray-haired sweethearts, tender and true,
　　Sharing life with its smiles and tears.

The flowery frocks and the ancient trunk,
　　And Grandmother Granger, too, are dust,
But something precious and sweet and rare
　　Survives the havoc of moth and rust;
Love with the wings of bright romance,
　　And the eyes of youth that are always gay—
Grandmother Granger's wedding gift
　　To every girl on her marriage day.

Wedding Feast

AMY BOWER

Just one more bride has passed before
The altar and out the old church door.
Her friends flung rice, her laugh was gay,
And merrily she was whisked away.

Then a brooding quiet settled down
On the dusty street in the little town;
And out from a nearby house there stole
A shabby old couple with broom and bowl.
They swept up the rice while their grateful faces
Blessed the bride in her silks and laces.

The Marriage Cake

UNKNOWN NINETEENTH-CENTURY ENGLISH POET

From the ends of the earth, from the ends of the earth,
Where the citrons are gold and the guava has birth,
Where the almond-boughs shed their soft blooms on the breeze,
And the lordliest fruit emblazon the trees,
We have run—we have rode—on winds vast and fleet,
To arrive in fit time with our treasure loads sweet,
That shall most powerful heighten, and heavenliest make
That glory of glories—the Bride's Marriage Cake!

We have searched out the sweet from its innermost fold—
We've the orange groves robbed of their ruddiest gold;
Our raisins we've chosen from the vine's sweetest clusters,
Which imbibed, as they dried, the sun's virtues and lustres.
We've the sweetest of spices to worthily make,
That glory of glories—the Bride's Marriage Cake.

Nor stay we—but, one and all, valiantly fling
In a glorious heap whatsoever he may bring:—
Be it sugars, or citrons, or perfumes, or spice,
Whatsoever is lusciously, fragrantly nice,
All to quickly compound, and triumphantly make,
That glory of glories—the Bride's Marriage Cake.

from **Wedding Gifts**

S. Y. AGNON

The magnate renowned, sire of the bride,
With his modest spouse, his crown and pride,
Shprintsa Pessil and Simeon Nathan,
Present to the bride and bridegroom one
Pair of candlesticks silver pure,
May their star shine bright and their star be sure,
While I the jester, Reb Joel hight,
Sing sweet song till Messiah's in sight.
To honor thee bridegroom, and thee O bride
As the sun and the moon so clear and bright,
And all who can sing will sing and cheer
Till the end of a hundred and twenty year.

The Wedding

Boris Pasternak

Across the courtyard
The wedding-guests stroll;
They have come with a concertina
To spend the night at the house of the bride.

Behind the host's doors,
Covered in thick felt,
From one in the morning 'til seven
The chatter is low and subdued.

But at dawn, when you sleep
Such a sleep that could last forever,
The accordion breaks in again,
The sound from the wedding.

And the musician begins again,
Strewing notes from the accordion all around,
Amid clapping of hands and flashes from necklaces,
In the din of the festivities.

Again, again, and again
Pounds the beat of the folk songs
Bursting into the sleepers in bed
From out of the merrymaking.

And one woman, as white as snow,
In the midst of the whistling and clamor,
Strikes out once again in a pea-hen step,
Moving rhythmically from side to side.

Her head keeps time with the beat
As her right hand throbs
All the while to the tune—
Pea-hen, pea-hen, pea-hen.

Then suddenly the gusto and noise of the playing,
The tread of the dancers in a ring,
Suddenly all falls to oblivion,
And sinks, as engulfed by water.

The noisy courtyard awakes;
A commonplace echo of business
Interrupts the conversation
And peals of laughter.

In the boundless sky above,
Flying like the wind are dove-blue patches—
A flock of doves rushing upwards,
Rushing upwards from the dove-cotes.

And to see them makes one feel,
In the trailing-off of the wedding,
Wishes for many years' happiness,
Sent out like doves on the wing.

Life itself is truly just a moment,
Only a dissolving
Of ourselves among all others,
As if we gave ourselves as gifts.

Only a wedding, only the depths of a window
That it breaks through from below;
Only a song, only a dream,
Only a blue dove.

Wedding Celebration

Tenrai Kono

The new couple is being united in the hall
    where the lights are shining brightly.
The people in the hall are listening
    to the notes of the wedding music.
The newlyweds are now in harmony,
    and the family will be prosperous.

Bridal Day

COMPTON MACKENZIE

This bridal day with gold I will enchain,
And wear its hours like rubies on my heart,
That you and I from Love may never part
Wile still these jeweled monuments remain.
These monuments, wrought out of hours, contain
The wound inflicted on me by Love's dart,
That stung with such intolerable smart,
Until to-day we vanquished Time and Pain.

And now I wear this crimson diadem
Where late my heart I did incarnadine
With open wounds in passionate array,
Unhealed until your eyes looked down at them,
And crystallized their sanguine drops to shine
In captured moments of our bridal day.

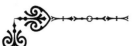

At the Wedding March

GERARD MANLEY HOPKINS

God with honor hang your head,
Groom, and grace you, bride, your bed
With lissome scions, sweet scions,
Out of hallowed bodies bred.

Each be other's comfort kind:
Deep, deeper than divined,
Divine charity, dear charity,
Fast you ever, fast bind.

Then let the March tread our ears:
I to him turn with tears
Who to wedlock, his wonder wedlock,
Deals triumph and immortal years.

Bride Waltz

Evert Taube

Sound accordion, clarinet, fiddles and flute—
Come and waltz with me, sweet, because you are so dear!
Only rarely one dances
At weddings and balls
With such sweet ladies as here in these halls.

But you are one of the few
Who are sweetest, it's true,
In this business of choosing I'm older than you.
For the sweetest brunette in the Nice carnival
Did a waltz once with Rönnerdahl!

Hush, the players have changed to a low, minor tune
That makes goblins and pixies dance under the moon.
And in meadows and fields round our house gay with light
Fairies dance in the dawning spring night.
Flowers cover the earth for our bride
Who expectantly blushing would hide.
Let us play, let us dream then where happiness dwells—
How our next meeting falls no one tells.

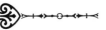

Wedding Song

Johann Wolfgang von Goethe

In nuptial chamber far from feast
Devoted Cupid keeps the watch
Lest wanton friends contrive some jest
Against the waiting bridal couch.
He waits for you. The torch's whorls
Encircle him, and golden flames
Impel the incense-scented mist
About the room in sensuous curls.

Your heart pounds when the hour sounds
That chases festive noises home,
Your eyes caress the lovely mouth
Now ever yours and yours alone.
You leave and guests, exclaiming, leave:
"Such joy be also ours, we pray."
The mother cries, and ever strict
Would even now keep you away.

To enter bliss complete and true
Love's sanctuary beckons you.
The torch, the waiting Cupid tries
To calm to gentle lamp, then his
To aid the bride's undressing.
Observing he's less deft than you,
He shyly turns and shields his eyes
And, smiling, gives his blessing.

from Old Senryū Collections

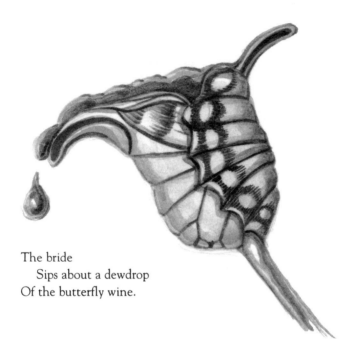

The bride
    Sips about a dewdrop
Of the butterfly wine.

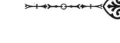

A Bride Song

CHRISTINA ROSSETTI

Through the vales to my love!
   To the happy small nest of home
Green from basement to roof;
   Where the honey-bees come
To the window-sill flowers,
   And dive from above,
Safe from the spider that weaves
   Her warp and her woof
In some outermost leaves.

Through the vales to my love!
   In sweet April hours
   All rainbows and flowers,
While dove answers dove,—
   In beautiful May,
When the orchards are tender
   And frothing with flowers,—
   In opulent June,
When the wheat stands up slender
   By sweet-smelling hay,
And half the sun's splendor
   Descends to the moon.

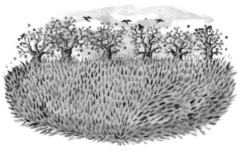

Through the vales to my love!
   Where the turf is so soft to the feet
   And the thyme makes it sweet,
And the stately foxglove
   Hangs silent its exquisite bells;
The greenness grows greener,
   And bulrushes stand
Round a lily to screen her.

Nevertheless, if this land,
   Like a garden to smell and to sight,
Was turned to a desert of sand;
   Strapped bare of delight,
   All its best gone to worst,
For my feet no repose,
   No water to comfort my thirst,
And heaven like a furnace above,—
   The desert would be
   As gushing of waters to me,
The wilderness be as a rose,
   If it led me to thee,
   O my love.

At the Savory Chapel

ROBERT GRAVES

Up to the wedding, formal with heirloom lace,
Press-cameras, carnations out of season,
Well-mellowed priest and well-trained choristers,

The relatives come marching, such as meet
Only at weddings and at funerals,
The elder generation with the eldest.

Family features for years undecided
What look to wear against a loveless world
Fix, as the wind veers, in the same grimace.

Each eyes the others with a furtive pity:
"Heavens, how she has aged—and he,
Gray hair and sunken cheeks, what a changed man!"

They stare wistfully at the bride (released
From brass buttons and the absurd salute)
In long white gown, bouquet and woman's pride.

"How suitable!" they whisper, and the whisper
"How suitable!" rustles from pew to pew;
To which I nod suitably grave assent.

Now for you, loving ones, who kneel at the altar
And preside afterwards at table—
The trophy sword that shears the cake recalling

What god you entertained last year together,
His bull neck looped with guts,
Trampling corpse-carpet through the villages—

Here is my private blessing: so to remain
As today you are, with features
Resolute and unchangeably your own.

On the Marriage of a Virgin

DYLAN THOMAS

Walking alone in a multitude of loves when morning's light
Surprised in the opening of her nightlong eyes
His golden yesterday asleep upon the iris
And this day's sun leapt up the sky out of her thighs
Was miraculous virginity old as loaves and fishes,
Though the moment of a miracle is unending lightning
And the shipyards of Galilee's footprints hide a navy of doves.

No longer will the vibrations of the sun desire on
Her deepsea pillow where once she married alone,
Her heart all ears and eyes, lips catching the avalanche
Of the golden ghost who ringed with his streams her mercury bone,
Who under the lids of her windows hoisted his golden luggage,
For a man sleeps where fire leapt down and she learns through his arm
That other sun, the jealous coursing of the unrivaled blood.

The Bride

EDITH SODERGRAN

My circle is narrow and the ring of my thoughts
goes round my finger.
There lies something warm at the base of all
                               strangeness around me,
like the vague scent in the water lily's cup,
thousands of apples hang in my father's garden,
round and completed in themselves—
my uncertain life turned out this way too,
shaped, rounded, bulging and smooth and
                               —simple.
Narrow is my circle and the ring of my thoughts
goes round my finger.

33

Marriage Song

William Thomas Walsh

You are more beautiful than light
    That trips across a waking lawn,
To pour on jonquils washed with night
    The hoarded prism of the dawn.

You are more lovely than the ray
    That trembles on a new-born leaf
When dusk steals on the drowsy day
    To gloat on beauty like a thief.

Since that white flaming speechless hour
    When vast and overshadowed wings
Housed you with Joy itself, the Power
    To whom its own perfection sings,

O bride of uncreated light,
    Caressed by love's infinity,
There dwells no dark in any night,
    No danger lurks on land or sea.

To My Bride

JÁNOS GARAY

I embrace you,
At last embrace you!
My burning love
Enchanting dew!

Your pretty eyes mine;
To see joy concealed,
To gaze into them—
Heaven is revealed.

Your little mouth mine,
Whose darling mistress,
Is loving tenderness
In her kiss.

Mine, your beautiful snow-
White breasts,
With noble, ardent
Feelings blessed.

From your eyes they
Flame into mine;
From your lips they
Kiss into mine;

Their benevolence
In your bosom is found—
Oh my lady, I'm
In your love bound.

And with this love
In paradise to be,
Is happiness eternally
Blooming for me.

POEMS

Oh lady, this sensation
So sweet, so great—
No, it's not a dream,
You are my sweet mate!

To the Bridegroom

UNKNOWN ANCIENT POET

A bowl full of ambrosia
now has been mixed,
and Hermes takes the wine jug
and pours for he gods.

Then all drain the wine cups
and make ritual libation,
portending for the bridegroom
all things that are good.

My Mayday Bride

VILHELM KRAG

My Mayday bride,
My Mayday bride!
The buttercups' petals are open wide,
They bow to the sun in festive pride,
While the May grass swings its lances.
And flower candles by the thousands
Light the hall of the earth with gold,
Where you will lead the dances.

My Mayday bride,
My Mayday bride!
I am the buttercup's heart so wide,
I wear the garment of passion's pride
To partner you on your way, love.
And born of my sorrow's crystal dew
Are the flowers of song I wove for you
To bind on your brow today, my love.

37

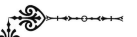

Ode to a Bridegroom

UNKNOWN MEDIEVAL POET

Rejoice, O bridegroom, in the wife of thy youth, thy comrade!
Let thy heart be merry now, and when thou shalt grow old
Sons to thy sons shalt thou see, thine old age's crown;
Sons who shall prosper and work in place of their pious sires.
Thy days in good shall be spent, thy years in pleasantness.
Floweth thy peace as a stream, riseth thy worth as its waves,
For peace shall be found in thy home, rest shall abide in thy dwelling.
Blessed be each day's work, blessed be thine all,
And thy bliss this assembly shall share, happy in thee.
By grace of us all ascend, thou and thy goodly company;
Rise we, too, to our feet, lovingly to greet thee;
One hope is now in all hearts, one prayer we utter,
Blessed be thy coming in, blessed be thy going forth.

The Bride

BELLA AKHMADULINA

Oh to be a bride
Brilliant in my curls
Under the white canopy
Of a modest veil!

How my hands tremble
Bound by my icy rings!
The glasses gather, brimming
With red compliments.

At last the world says yes;
It wishes me roses and sons.
My friends stand shyly at the door,
Carrying love gifts.

Chemises in cellophane,
Plates, flowers, lace...
They kiss my cheeks, they marvel
I'm to be a wife.

Soon my white gown
Is stained with wine like blood;
I feel both lucky and poor
As I sit, listening, at the table.

Terror and desire
Loom in the forward hours.
My mother, the darling, weeps—
Mama is like the weather.

...My rich, royal attire
I lay aside on the bed.
I find I am afraid
To look at you, to kiss you.

Loudly the chairs are set
Against the wall, eternity...
My love, what more can happen
To you and to me?

translated by Stephen Stepanchev

Chosen of Bridegrooms

JUDAH HALEVI

Carry your greeting to the chosen of bridegrooms
And his loved ones and faithful friends—
The greeting of a lover who overcomes the distance with his eyes,
And sees with his heart, face to face.
Children of nobles, plants of loveliness
Whose faces give light through the marriage bower
Like stars through the thickness of clouds.

To the Bride

UNKNOWN ANCIENT POET

Bride, so filled with rosy longings,
Bride, fair ornament of Love's queen,
Come now to nuptial couch,
Come now to bed, to sweet and gentle sport,
To your bridegroom, come.

Full willing,
You shall find the path
With evening star as guide
To Matrimony's silver throne
And wedlock's wonder.

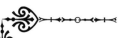

The Worn Wedding-Ring

WILLIAM COX BENNETT

Your wedding-ring wears thin, dear wife; ah, summers not a few,
Since I put it on your finger first, have passed o'er me and you;
And love, what changes we have seen, what cares and pleasures, too,—
Since you became my own dear wife, when this old ring was new!

O, blessings on that happy day, the happiest of my life,
When, thanks to God, your low, sweet "Yes" made you my loving wife!
Your heart will say the same, I know; that day's as dear to you,—
That day that made me yours, dear wife, when this old ring was new.

How well do I remember now your young sweet face that day!
How fair you were, how dear you were, my tongue could hardly say;
Nor how I doted on you; O, how proud I was of you!
But did I love you more than now, when this old ring was new?

No—no! No fairer were you then that at this hour to me;
And, dear as life to me this day, how could you dearer be?
As sweet your face might be that day as now it is, 'tis true;
But did I know your heart as well when this old ring was new?

O partner of my gladness, wife, what care, what grief is there
For me you would not bravely face, with me you would not share?
O, what a weary want had every day if wanting you,
Wanting the love that God made mine when this old ring was new!

Yours bring fresh links to bind us, wife,—young voices that are here;
Young faces round our fire that make our mother's yet more dear;
Young loving hearts your care each day makes yet more like to you,
More like the loving heart made mine when this old ring was new.

And blessed be God! All he has given are with us yet; around
Our table every precious life lent to us still is found.
Though cares we've known, with hopeful hearts the worst we've
    struggled through;
Blessed be his name for all his love since this old ring was new!

The past is dear, its sweetness still our memories treasure yet;
The griefs we've borne, together borne, we would not now forget.
Whatever, wife, the future brings, heart unto heart still true,
We'll share as we have shared all else since this old ring was new.

And if God spare us 'mongst our sons and daughters to grow old,
We know his goodness will not let your heart or mine grow cold.
Your aged eyes will see in mine all they've still shown to you,
And mine in yours all they have seen since this old ring was new.

And O, when death shall come at last to bid me to my rest,
May I die looking in those eyes, and resting on that breast;
O, may my parting gaze be blessed with the dear sight of you,
Of those fond eyes,—fond as they were when this old ring was new!

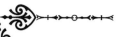

Of the Night, Let the Bridegroom Sing

STATIUS

As day dawns bright by Heaven's grace,
The bridegroom walks the clouds
And roams the shining sky,
But it seems to him the stars stand still
And slow Aurora tarries.

Witnesses of the wooing,
The hills and shores and woods
Echo the bridal songs
While poet-friends bear gifts
To their loved fellow bard.
One brings a lyre, one his wands,
And one the tawny skin of spotted deer.
One brings a quill to strike the lyre,
One rings the poet's brow with bays,
And one with Ariadne's crown.

The day has scarce begun
Amid auguries of bliss
When both homes are astir with festal company.
The gates are green with leaves,
The crossways bright with fire
And gay robes hedged about
With folk in plain attire.
The company envies man and maid,
But the bridegroom more.

In the gateway Hymen stands
Composing a new bridal song
To bewitch the poet-bridegroom.
Juno blesses the nuptial knot
And Concord unites the throng.

Such is the wedding day.
Of the night, let the bridegroom sing.

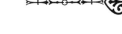

this little bride & groom are

e. e. eummings

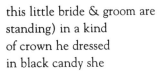

this little bride & groom are
standing) in a kind
of crown he dressed
in black candy she

veiled with candy white
carrying a bouquet of
pretend flowers this
candy crown with this candy

little bride & little
groom in it kind of stands on a much
less thin very much more

big & kinder of ring & which
kinder of stands on a
much more than very much
biggest & thickest & kindest

of ring & all one two three rings
are cake & everything is protected by
cellophane against anything (because
nothing really exists

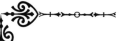

To My Dear and Loving Husband

ANNE BRADSTREET

If ever two were one, then surely we;
If ever man were loved by wife, then thee;
If ever wife was happy in a man,
Compare with me, ye woman, if you can.
I prize thy love more than whole mines of gold,
Or all the riches that the East doth hold.
My love is such that rivers cannot quench,
Nor ought but love from thee give recompense.
Thy love is such I can no way repay;
The heavens regard thee manifold, I pray.
Then while we live in love let's so persevere
That when we live no more we may live ever.

The Rain's Marriage

MARCIA SOUTHWICK

In an African folk tale, the rain
falls in love with a blacksmith.
At the wedding, the downpour dies
     out
to a single stream, a column of water.
As the first drop touches soil,
feet appear, then legs, a torso, arms....
The woman, waves of transparent hair
falling over her shoulders, is called
the *Water Bride* and doesn't fully lose
her identity as rain. Once,
I was certain of the boundaries
     between my body
and whatever it touched, as if
touch itself were a way of defining
     exactly where *I* stopped
and the rest of the world began.
Then I lost the sense that I was
     hemmed in
by skin. My body felt like something
     loaned to me—
it might break, or dissolve to ashes,
leaving me stranded,
a pure thought without a skull to
     inhabit—
like rain falling into any shape that
     accepts it,
every hollow place made equal by its touch.
The mind of rain
contemplates even the smallest crack in the parched dirt
where nothing will grow.
Why can't I fall effortlessly in love?

If I knew the exact place where my body stops
and everything else begins, I'd marry.
Like the *Water Bride*, I'd be unafraid,
though surely trouble would exist, as between rain
and a blacksmith's fire.

Any Wife or Husband

Carol Haynes

Let us be guests in one another's house
With deferential "No" and courteous "Yes";
Let us take care to hide our foolish moods
Behind a certain show of cheerfulness.

Let us avoid all sullen silences;
We should find fresh and sprightly things to say;
I must be fearful lest you find me dull,
And you must dread to bore me any way.

Let us knock gently at each other's heart,
Glad of a chance to look within—and yet
Let us remember that to force one's way
Is the unpardoned breach of etiquette.

So shall I be hostess—you, the host—
Until all need for entertainment ends;
We shall be lovers when the last door shuts,
But what is better still—we shall be friends.

Man and Wife

Shin Shalom

I wed you not with overwhelming lyre,
　　You won me by assurance deep and calm.
　　Our love-song was enhanced by wisdom's psalm,
　　You gave me all the light and hid the fire.

　　My soul was snugly sheltered in your palm
　　From staying wild, from deviation's briar;
　　And when despair would tempt me to retie,
　　Your tact and taste endowed me their balm.

　　How good to lean my head against your breast,
　　The warp of sorrow and the woof of joy
　　To weave around your heart in peace and rest.

　　With me you are—who will my lot destroy?
　　With you I am—sleep on, beloved name.
　　I guard your altar, keep the sacred flame.

translated by Abraham Birman

Happy Marriage

Thomas Blacklock

Thou genius of connubial love, attend!
Let silent wonder all thy powers suspend,
Whilst to thy glory I devote my lays,
And pour forth all my grateful heart in praise.
    In lifeless strains let vulgar satire tell
That marriage oft is mixed with heaven and hell,
That conjugal delight is soured with spleen,
And peace and war compose the varied scene.
My muse a truth sublimer can assert,
And sing the triumphs of a mutual heart.
    Thrice happy they who through life's varied tide
With equal pace and gentle motion glide,
Whom, though the wave of fortune sinks or swells,
One reason governs and one wish impels,
Whose emulation is to love the best,
Who feels no bliss but in each other blest,
Who knows no pleasure but the joys they give,
Nor cease to love but when they cease to live.
If fate these blessings in one lot combine,
Then let the' eternal page record them mine.

The Marriage

Yvor Winters

Incarnate for our marriage you appeared,
Flesh living in the spirit and endeared
By minor graces and slow sensual change.
Through every nerve we made our spirits range.
We fed our minds on every mortal thing:
The lacy fronds of carrots in the spring,
Their flesh sweet on the tongue, the salty wine
From bitter grapes, which fathered through the vine
The mineral drought of autumn concentrate,
Wild spring in dream escaping, the debate
Of flesh and spirit on those vernal nights,
Its resolution in naïve delights,
The young kids bleating softly in the rain—
All this to pass, not to return again.
And when I found your flesh did not resist,
It was the living spirit that I kissed,
It was the spirit's change in which I lay:
Thus, mind in mind we waited for the day.
When flesh shall fall away, and, falling, stand
Wrinkling with shadow over face and hand,
Still I shall meet you on the verge of dust
And know you as a faithful vestige must.
And, in commemoration of our lust,
May our heirs seal us in a single urn,
A single spirit never to return.

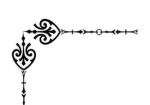

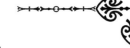

Wedding Pillow

Kim Sowol

Jaw clenched
at thoughts of death.
Moonlight dapples
the windowsill.

In unsettled sleep
tears drench the pillowing arm.
An insomniac pheasant
cries in the night.

The floating moon pillow—
Where does it lie?
On the pillow where two once slept
was a vow made for life and death?

In spring the cuckoo
by the foot of the hill
will cry enough,
my love… my love.

The floating moon pillow—
Where does it lie?
Moonlight dapples the windowsill.

The Moon's Bed, the Bride's Bed

W. S. Rendra

The moon's bed, the bride's bed:
An azure blue sky
Held up by ancient hands;
A cricket flutters about,
Shrilling a love song to the net.

The moon's bed, the bride's bed:
A Chinese junk with a thousand sails
Crossing the sea of sleep;
Stars fall one by one,
Yawning with sweet visions.

The moon's bed, the bride's bed:
A kingdom of ghosts and spirits,
Drunk with the flavor of incense;
Dreams scatter, one by one,
Cracked by brittle truth.

The moon's bed, the bride's bed:
The harsh earth of reality
That pleasure and hope had concealed;
Dry soil toiled over,
Seeded, made fertile.

The moon's bed, the bride's bed:
An ivory bed,
A porcelain and china bed,
A marble and alabaster bed,

A stone bed,
A wind-blown bed,
Paved with asphalt:
Newly-weds swallowing life,
Eye to eye, hand in hand.

Marriage Poem

Sapardi Djoko Damono

Whose is it, this light?
(the petals of the night
fall) the horizon glooms
in the room, in Lovemaking

grain by grain
(You and I, I
and the pollen of the night) slide
unite

Marriage which is placeless, time
-less
petal by petal opened
perfect night

from **Paradise Lost, Book Five**

JOHN MILTON

Here Love his golden shafts employs, here lights
His constant lamp, and waves his purple wings,
Reigns here and revels; not in the bought smile
Of harlots—loveless, joyless, unendeared,
Casual fruition; nor in court amours,
Mixed dance, or wanton mask, or midnight ball,
Or serenade, which the starved lover sings
To his proud fair, best quitted with disdain.
These, lulled by nightingales, embracing slept,
And on their naked limbs the flowery roof
Showered roses, which the morn repaired. Sleep on,
Blest pair! and, O! yet happiest, if ye seek
No happier state, and know to know no more!

Quotations

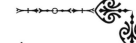

The Wedding Celebration

To have and to hold, from this day forward, for better or for worse,
for richer for poorer, in sickness and in health, to love and to
cherish, till death us do part.

—THE BOOK OF COMMON PRAYER

Let all thy joys be as the month of May
And all thy days be as a marriage day.

—FRANCIS QUARLES (1594–1644)

Hail wedded love, mysterious law, true source
Of human offspring, sole propriety,
In Paradise of all things common else.

—JOHN MILTON

QUOTATIONS

If a bride can't dance,
she claims the musicians can't play.

—YIDDISH PROVERB

I sing of brooks, of blossoms, birds, and bowers:
Of April, May, of June, and July flowers.
I sing of Maypoles, hock-carts, wassail, wakes,
Of bridegrooms, brides, and of their bridal cakes.

—ROBERT HERRICK (1591–1674)

There is something about a wedding-gown
Prettier than any other gown in the world.

—DOUGLAS JERROLD (1803–1857)

Every wedding where true lovers wed, helps on the march of universal Love.
Who are brides here shall be Love's bridesmaids in the marriage world to come.

—HERMAN MELVILLE (1819–1891)

There's as much difference in wedding rings as there is in wedding people.

—GEORGE MEREDITH (1828–1909)

The bridegroom and bride are one, the people of the procession—outsiders.

—MARATHI PROVERB

When the wedding march sounds the resolute approach, the clock no longer ticks; it tolls the hour.... The figures in the aisle are no longer individuals; they symbolize the human race.

—ANNE MORROW LINDBERGH (B. 1906)

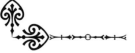

The voice that breathed o'er Eden,
That earliest wedding-day,
The primal marriage blessing,
It hath not passed away.

—JOHN KEBLE (1792–1866)

What can we do but rejoice with a triumphing bridegroom and bride?

—SIR JOHN BETJEMAN (1906–1984)

That is a wise regulation of the Church which makes the marriage ceremony brief, for the intensity of the feelings it often creates would frequently become too powerful to be suppressed, were it unnecessarily prolonged.

—JAMES FENIMORE COOPER (1789–1851)

When the wedding is over, the little boxes of makeup are missing. [At Hindu weddings many little things disappear.]

—TAMIL PROVERB

The evening is a black bride
wearing silver necklaces.

—AL-MA 'ARRI

If fruit could be had in November, weddings would be solemnized even then.

—Tamil Proverb

My marriage was much the most fortunate and joyous event which happened to me in the whole of my life.

—Winston Churchill (1871–1947)

The wedding vow is a short prologue to a long drama.

—Hebrew Proverb

Those two falling in love let them become one,
Let them in vain not spill the holy wine.

—Maximilian Voloshin

Quotations

Parents can give a dowry but not luck.

—YIDDISH PROVERB

The supreme and overmastering desire of any two humans who are in love with one another is to be together and alone, in a shared and mutual solitude. That (in much) is what weddings are for. It is attained and safeguarded in marriage. How well and happily then should it be spoken of, how profound should be its appeal to our common humanity.

—WALTER DE LA MARE (1873–1956)

Advice for the Newlyweds

In matters of religion and matrimony
I never give any advice, because I will not
have anybody's torments in this world or the
next laid to my charge.

—LORD CHESTERFIELD (1694–1773)

A person's character is but half formed till after wedlock.

—C. E. SIMMONS (1879–1952)

He who marries *might* be sorry. He who does not *will* be sorry.

—CZECH PROVERB

When ye unite with another, do so with deep consciousness of the greatness of the dignity of that which you do! Give yourself to this work of love; with your souls and with your minds, even as with your flesh.

—OMAR HALEBY

The bridge between 'single' and 'married' spans life's most crucial Rubicon. It is one singularly easy to cross, but not to retraverse. No other venture in life promises so much, may achieve even more, or prove so disastrous.

—WALTER DE LA MARE (1873–1956)

- One should believe in marriage as in the immortality of the soul.

—HONORÉ DE BALZAC (1799–1850)

- A perfect marriage is a hearth and a horizon.

—ELIZABETH ASQUITH BIBESCO (1897–1945)

- A successful marriage is an edifice that must be rebuilt every day.

—ANDRÉ MAUROIS (1885–1967)

A good marriage is that in which each appoints the other guardian of his solitude. Once the realization is accepted that even between the closest human beings infinite distances continue to exist, a wonderful living side by side can grow up, if they succeed in loving the distance between them which makes it possible to see the other whole and against a wide sky.

—RAINER MARIA RILKE (1921–1985)

• The happiness of married life depends upon making small sacrifices with readiness and cheerfulness.

—JOHN SELDON (1584–1654)

• One year of Joy, another of Comfort, the rest of Content, make the married life happy.

—THOMAS FULLER (1654–1734)

• Often the difference between a successful marriage and a mediocre one consists of leaving about three or four things a day unsaid.

—HARLAN MILLER (1880–1926)

Estimate her by the qualities she has,
and not by the qualities she may not have.
This is marriage.

—CHARLES DICKENS (1812–1870)

Pains do not hold a marriage together. It is threads, hundreds of tiny threads which sew people together through the years.

—SIMONE SIGNORET (1921–1985)

Marriage is not a finished affair. No matter to what age you live, love must be continuously consolidated. Being considerate, thoughtful, and respectful without ulterior motives is the key to a good marriage.

—PAMPHLET FROM THE CHINESE FAMILY PLANNING CENTER

If you are afraid of loneliness, don't marry.

—ANTON CHEKHOV (1860–1904)

A man too good for the world is no good for his wife.

—Yiddish proverb

There are millions of people today who never could marry happily—however favorable the conditions might be—simply because their natures do not contain in sufficient strength the elements of loving surrender to one another.

—Edward Carpenter (1872–1950)

A marriage is like a long trip in a tiny rowboat: if one passenger starts to rock the boat, the other has to steady it; other wise, they will go to the bottom together.

—David R. Reuben (b. 1933)

A forced marriage doesn't bear good fruit.

—Yiddish proverb

Quotations

(If there is one thing a couple should not do,
it is to work at the relationship as though it were some kind of task.

—WILLIAM MASTERS (B. 1915) AND VIRGINIA JOHNSON (B. 1925)

(Hasty marriage seldom proveth well.

—WILLIAM SHAKESPEARE (1564–1616)

After marriage arrives a reaction, sometimes a big, sometimes a little one; but it comes sooner or later, and must be tided over by both parties if they desire the rest of their lives to go with the current.

—RUDYARD KIPLING (1865–1936)

Marriage, building a pagoda, and tattooing are three undertakings which, once embarked upon, can only be altered later with great difficulty.

—MYANMAR PROVERB

Marriage is a union founded on free and mutual consent. It cannot exist without friendship. It cannot exist without personal fidelity.

—CHARLES BROCKDEN BROWN (1771–1810)

We should marry to please ourselves, not other people.

—ISAAC BICKERSTAFFE (1733–1808)

Among unequals what society can sort, what harmony, or true delight?

—JOHN MILTON (1608–1674)

Not the marriage of convenience, nor the marriage of reason, but the marriage of love. All other marriage, with vows so solemn, with intimacy so close, is but acted falsehood and varnished sin.

—EDWARD ROBERT BULWER (1831–1891)

To give delight, marriage must join two minds.

—LORD BROOKE (1883–1963)

If you would marry suitably, marry your equal.

—OVID (43 B.C.–A.D. 18)

(The only thing that can hallow marriage is love, and the only genuine
  marriage is that which is hallowed by love.

—LEO TOLSTOY (1828–1910)

Where there's marriage without love,
there will be love without marriage.

—BENJAMIN FRANKLIN (1706–1790)

Never marry but for love; but see that thou lovest what is lovely.

—WILLIAM PENN (1644–1718)

In marriage reverence is more important even than love....
A steady awareness in each that the other has a kinship with the eternal.

—FRED J. SHIELD (1904–1970)

Of love and marriage, coarse men speak with sneers and obscene jests, while serious men express themselves in hints, with apologetic smiles, as if they were betraying a weakness.

—HAMLIN GARLAND (1860–1940)

QUOTATIONS

Humorous

The world has grown suspicious of anything that looks like a happily married life.

—OSCAR WILDE (1854–1900)

Marriage is popular because it combines the maximum of temptation with the maximum of opportunity.

—GEORGE BERNARD SHAW (1856–1950)

If it were not for the presents, an elopement would be preferable.

—GEORGE ADE (1866–1944)

One doesn't have to get anywhere in a marriage. It's not a public conveyance.

—IRIS MURDOCH (B. 1919)

I love to cry at weddings, anybody's weddings anytime!… anybody's weddings just so long as it's not mine!

—DOROTHY FIELDS (1905–1974)

The great secret of a successful marriage is to treat all disasters as incidents and none of the incidents as disasters.

—HAROLD NICOLSON (1886–1968)

'What are your views on marriage?'
'Rather garbled.'

—NOËL COWARD (1899–1973)

Did you ever look through a microscope at a drop of pond water? You see plenty of love there. All the amoebae getting married. I presume they think it very exciting and important. We don't.

—ROSE MACAULAY (1881–1958)

Marriage isn't a word... it's a *sentence*!

—KING VIDOR (1895–1982)

When two people are under the influence of the most violent, most insane, most delusive, and most transient of passions, they are required to swear that they will remain in that excited, abnormal, and exhausting condition continuously until death do them part.

—GEORGE BERNARD SHAW (1856–1950)

One of the best things about marriage is that it gets young people to bed at a decent hour.

—MERLE McNEIL MUSSELMAN (1915–1990)

I am not against hasty marriages,
where a mutual flame is fanned by an adequate income.

—WILKIE COLLINS (1824–1889)

Marriage probably has the poorest public relations of any institution in the world, but its business is only slightly short of spectacular.

—DOUGLAS MEADOR (B. 1937)

The value of marriage is not that adults produce children
but that children produce adults.

—PETER DE VRIES (1910–1993)

So that is marriage, Lily thought, a man and a woman looking at a
girl throwing a ball.

—VIRGINIA WOOLF (1882–1941)

Propitious Days for Weddings:
Monday for wealth,
Tuesday for health,
Wednesday the best day of all;
Thursday for crosses,
Friday for losses,
Saturday no luck at all.

—ANONYMOUS

QUOTATIONS

So sweet was the toad's husband,
that ever since her wedding she's carried him on her back.

—NIGERIAN PROVERB

A married couple are well suited when both partners usually feel
the need for a quarrel at the same time.

—JEAN ROSTAND (1894–1977)

It feels so fine to be a bride,
And how's the groom? Why he's slightly fried,
It's delightful, it's delicious, it's de-lovely.

—COLE PORTER (1891–1964)

A woman whose dresses are made in Paris and whose marriage has been made in Heaven might be equally biased for and against free imports.

—SAKI [H. H. MUNRO] (1870–1916)

On the whole, I haven't found men unduly loath to say, 'I love you.' The real trick is to get them to say, 'Will you marry me?'

—ILKA CHASE (1903–1978)

Every woman should marry an archaeologist because she grows increasingly attractive to him as she grows increasingly to resemble a ruin.

—AGATHA CHRISTIE (1890–1976)

(I am about to be married—and am of course in all the misery of a man in pursuit of happiness.

—LORD BYRON (1788–1824)

"Let's get married or something."
"We'll get married or nothing."

—ANONYMOUS

I would be married, but I'd have no wife:
I would be married to a single life.

—RICHARD CRASHAW (1613–1649)

(To keep your marriage brimming
With love in the loving cup,
Whenever you're wrong, admit it,
Whenever you're right, shut up.

—OGDEN NASH (1902–1957)

Surnames to be avoided in marriage:
To change the name, and not the letter,
Is a change for the worse, and not for the better.

—ANONYMOUS

The critical period in matrimony is breakfast time.

—A. P. HERBERT (1890–1971)

A simple enough pleasure, surely, to have breakfast alone with one's husband,
but how seldom married people in the midst of life achieve it.

—ANNE MORROW LINDBERGH (B. 1906)

QUOTATIONS

Wedding Anniversaries

1ST — Cotton

2ND — Paper

3RD — Leather

4TH — Flower

5TH — Wooden

6TH — Iron

7TH — Woolen

8TH — Bronze

9TH — Copper

10TH — Tin

11TH — Steel

12TH — Silk

13TH — Lace

15TH — Crystal

25TH — Silver

30TH — Pearl

35TH — Coral

40TH — Ruby

45TH — Sapphire

50TH — Golden

55TH — Emerald

60TH — Diamond

 Short Stories

The Wedding

Fyodor Dostoevsky

As I was passing by a particular church a few days back, I was surprised to see a huge crowd and a large number of carriages. Everyone around me was talking about a wedding. The day was overcast—it was beginning to sleet. I followed the crowd into the church and saw the bridegroom. He was a round, sleek little man with a belly, elaborately adorned. He was restless, at once in every part of the church, attending to everything and giving orders. Then a rumor spread through the crowd that the bride had finally arrived. I pushed my way through the people and saw an extraordinarily beautiful girl for whom the blossoming spring of life had scarcely begun. But the beautiful girl was sad and pale. She looked about without interest—I even fancied that her eyes were red from tears. The classic severity of every feature of her face contributed a touch of solemn dignity to her beauty. And through this severity and dignity, through this sadness, a faint glimmer of the first innocent blooming of childhood could still be discerned. The sensation I received was of something incredibly naive, of something unfinished, something young and fresh, and of something, too, that seemed mutely beseeching mercy.

People whispered that she was only sixteen. Looking closely at the bridegroom, I recognized in a flash Julian Mastakovich. I looked back at her—dear God!...

I began to make my way quickly to the door. In the crowd they were saying that the bride was an heiress, that her dowry was worth five hundred thousand, not to mention the thousands that must have been spent on her trousseau....

"He got his sum right, by God," I thought as I elbowed my way into the street.

SHORT STORIES

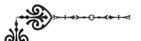

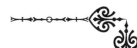

The Marriage Feast

Pär Lagerkvist

Jonas and Frida were to be married at four o'clock in the afternoon, and the guests were beginning to collect at the little house on the outskirts of the village by the railway where the ceremony was to take place. Ponies and traps came from the surrounding countryside, where one or two distant relatives of Frida lived—Jonas hadn't any—and there were also several people from the village itself. It seemed that they would be about fifteen, all told.

It was a lovely day and the men were outside, strolling in the little garden, shaking hands with each other, standing talking, or taking a turn around the house as though they were looking it over. On the east gable was a faded sign over a small doorway:

Frida Johansson
Haberdasher

Hm. Well, well, so Frida was getting off today. Aha. That was all they said, but their tone implied plenty.

Hm, it was a funny thing about this wedding, but there would be the usual food and drink anyway, and they might just as well be there, seeing they were invited. So they thought about going in.

The bridegroom was standing on the steps. He was a thick-set, insignificant little man, with a fair, drooping mustache and a continual happy smile—he was always smiling. He had clear, kind, almost grateful eyes, and he blinked a lot, almost as though to keep out of the way. He was apt to hold his head rather on one side, as if he were listening. He had a very pleasing appearance, he had indeed. His real name was Jonas Samuelsson; but he was usually called Jonas Gate, owing to his habit of always hanging about down by the level-crossing gate in his younger days, in case anyone off the train wanted a hand with the luggage. It had thus been quite some time before he had turned his hand to any steady job, but he had been porter at the hotel for a long time now, so his standing down by the level-crossing gate was all in order. It was his profession. As to that, of course, he was going to marry Frida today, so it was harder now to say what he was, or thought of being: whether he would help her in the shop if need be, or even give up work altogether. There was no telling what Frida's plans were, or how much she had been able to scrape together. No one had any idea. Maybe it was quite a tidy sum. But she might just as well let him stay on down there, it suited him somehow. He wasn't a particularly go-ahead chap.

The relatives didn't really like the idea of Frida getting married in this way, and it wasn't surprising. Not that they cared what she let herself in for—that was her lookout. But there was no need to go and get married at her age; it was unnecessary, they thought. And she had always been one to save a bit—not that *they* knew anything about that, it had nothing to do with them. But now that she was going to at last, she might have chosen someone other than Jonas. Not that there were so many to choose from. But Frida was one of them, after all, and came from a good family, so it did seem strange that she could put up with him. Well, well, that was her business; she wanted it that way. He was certainly a nice, good-natured sort of chap, that he was. No one could say he wasn't.

Jonas was standing on the porch receiving the guests and looking around obligingly as though wondering if there were something he could carry. And if someone arrived with a coat that he had had on in the gig, or with anything at all, he was delighted to help carry it in. It was something he could do, and on a day like this a man is only too glad to show what he is capable of. It was worse once all the guests had arrived, for no one spoke to him and he just stood there, still smiling, with his arms hanging beside his new black suit, which Frida had had made for the occasion. He had nothing in particular to do, but as usual he looked contented all the same.

It was better after awhile when it was time for coffee and he could find chairs for everyone and beamingly invite them to sit at the table. He said nothing; he preferred to speak only when he had to. He did think of asking them to be sure and have more buns and cakes, but he thought better of it; they were Frida's after all. The guests helped themselves all the same, and over their second cups began talking and feeling more at home. Jonas was delighted; he stood beside the mantelpiece with his cup of coffee, listening to all that was said with the most heartfelt goodwill; ran out into the kitchen to fill the coffeepot, handed the sugar around to the women at the tables by the window, and generally made himself useful. Of course, it wasn't usual for the bridegroom to do the waiting like that, but he probably

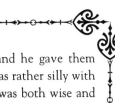

didn't know. They smiled at him in their own way, and he gave them his sweet smile in return. They may have thought he was rather silly with that smile of his, but one couldn't say that, because it was both wise and kind. It was just that he never stopped smiling. Well, that was his way. He was thinking now how well it was all going; it was too—there wasn't a hitch.

 Up in the attic Frida was sitting being dressed as a bride. Agnes Karlsson, her best friend as they say, was pinching Frida's thin hair around the tongs so that there was a smell of burning right out through the window. It was the first time Frida had had her hair curled, but then it was the thing to do. She hardly recognized herself as she looked in the bureau mirror that she had had moved up. She was not very like the old Frida, which was as it should be on such a festive day.

Oh, just think of its being today! Today that she and Jonas were to stand in front of the altar and be joined in matrimony forever and ever before their God. To think that that day was really here, and that it was to happen soon, in a little while.

"I hope they have arranged the flowers properly down there, as I said, beside the stools. Do you think they have, Agnes?"

"Oh yes, they'll have done that all right."

"And do you think the wedding cake has arrived safely, the one with our initials?"

"Yes, it's sure to have come. I saw Klas arriving with a cake box—that was probably it."

"Supposing you were to go down just to make sure?"

"Good heavens, we must get this finished."

"Yes, of course, that's very important. Everything is important on a day like this; one must think of everything."

Oh, if only everything goes off all right, and it's the kind of festival she has hoped for, that she has dreamed about so much. If only it's all as the great solemnity of the occasion demands.

What is there on earth greater than two people being made one, meeting before God to have their compact sealed at the throne of the Eternal One? Alas, there were no doubt many who never gave a thought to what kind of festival this really was, looked on it as a gay party where

 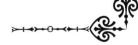

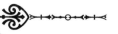

they could dance and laugh. Which it was as well; of course, she herself was so happy that she was dancing inside. No bride could be happier than she, and none had more reason to be. No, none.

And yet, in spite of everything, in spite of all this joy—it was nevertheless the solemnity she felt most of all. The great solemnity that lay over this day of theirs. What they were now faced with was the most momentous thing that could happen to her and Jonas. Their lives were to be united, they were to be made one, their souls were to be joined together forever. Neither of them would be lonely anymore, neither she nor Jonas. How strange it was, never to be lonely anymore. She knew what it meant, she who had been alone ever since her parents died when she was a child. She had been made to know so well what it was, every day of her life. No, it is not good for man to live alone.

Was it strange then, that at this glorious moment she wanted everything to be as worthy and beautiful as possible?

"Take a look in the mirror and see what you think," Agnes said.

And Frida leaned forward and looked at her reflection, stroked her forehead, touched her unfamiliar hair.

How small and thin her face was; she looked like a girl with anemia. But her features were worn and her cheeks were sunken. The years had put their mark upon her, she had so many wrinkles; but it was all so delicate and fine, it all seemed to have been carefully done. Even a scar on her neck seemed small and delicate, like everything else about her. Only her eyes were large, infinitely gentle and artless, and strangely wide open. Her mouth looked like a thin line, as though she had been a very determined and enterprising woman, but that was only because it was so thin and just as pale as the rest. It was when she smiled that it became transformed. It was extraordinary; her whole face lit up at once. Also she had the nicest false teeth in the whole district; there were many who thought so if it came to that. They fitted so well.

No, she was not beautiful. She never had been and now it was no longer to be expected. But there was something unusually pure about her, as is often the way with seamstresses and laundresses. She had done sewing for many years before setting up her shop, and there, too, she always had to do with clean and delicate things. She was so well-suited to them, which is probably why she had taken to it. Her hands were quite white, since she had never had to do any rough work, but she had worked hard with them just the same; one could see that.

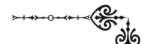

"What about trying on the coronet," Agnes said, "So that we can see if the hair suits it? You say you want to have it."

"Yes, Agnes dear, do."

So Agnes fastened it onto the top of Frida's head with hairpins, a little coronet of myrtle which Frida had woven so neatly out of a myrtle she had inherited from her mother, who had used it when she was a bride. Three times it had died out, but she had taken cuttings, so it was the same tree really. The inside of the coronet was filled with white tulle, which billowed out in a lovely veil.

Frida stood up to see herself properly in the mirror. She had not yet put on her petticoat and dress, in order not to crease them, but her drawers were snow white and trimmed with the finest lace in the whole shop; the veil fell light and airy down her back, right to her knees. She was really very sweet standing there admiring herself, so thoughtful and happy. She looked at her reflection with dreamy eyes, seeing herself for the first time as a bride.

"You've nothing on but your drawers!" Agnes exclaimed, and burst out laughing.

She hadn't, either. Frida smiled gently as she realized it, then held the veil aside and carefully sat down again.

Agnes thought the coronet was too flat on the head.

"No, do you think so? I hadn't thought of it. Yes, perhaps it's not quite right."

"Supposing we curled the hair a bit more, so that it sits a little higher? But it's not so easy to get it up any higher, you see."

"No, it's so thin, isn't it?"

"Yes, that's just the trouble, but I'll have a try."

So Agnes very kindly started all over again; she took hair from the sides and got it up on top, although it wouldn't really reach, and then had the idea of putting the knot up there, too, for it didn't matter where it was, seeing that the veil would hide it anyway. She was so kind and helpful.

And during all this Frida sat there in a dream, which was not strange....

She was thinking of how she and Jonas had met, how their destinies had been linked together, their steps guided forward to this great and glorious hour. They had been fond of each other for a long, long time, goodness knows how many years. It was a secret harmony of their souls, without words, without their being aware of it themselves. It had not blossomed into real love until later on, but they had, as it were, come closer to one another, even so. She remembered how he had taken her suitcase once when she had come off the train from town. They had walked along the street and he had said, "I suppose you have been in to do some shopping," and she had said, "Yes, I have," but as she said it she had happened to look into his eyes. That was four years ago now, but she remembered as though it were yesterday. That was when it had started in earnest.

Yes, how strange everything is, people's destinies—what is it that guides us? What had brought her and Jonas together to this sacred feeling that they would never be parted again?

But still a long time passed before there was anything said between them. That's the way of it. Oh, this deceptive game of love, this sweet game of hide-and-seek played by two people in love. The feelings of both are the same, but neither will admit it. Their souls are drawn to each other, reach out to each other in ardent longing, call to each other like twittering birds, like animals in their stalls in the evening.

And mixed up with it all a constantly disquieting uneasiness, in spite of everything. I suppose he does love me. Perhaps he doesn't. And do I really love him, with all my heart, deep down inside, as one should? As one must? Is it ordained by God that we are two souls meant to meet during our wandering here, to enter into the shining abode of love? Are we chosen and fit for it? Yes, yes, I will believe, I will believe!

Yes, she believed. She knew. She sat gazing in front of her in tranquil rapture, transported by happiness.

No, no two people on earth could have met in a nicer, more beautiful way than they had, she and Jonas. Her eyes grew moist as she thought of it, and her gaze grew remote as though she were looking at a far-off land.

Was she right? Yes, that's how it was; what they felt for each other was love. She had accepted him because she was fond of him. She loved for the sake of loving. And Jonas? He had said yes because he thought it was so boundlessly good of her to accept him. He had never imagined it; but as

soon as he was allowed to, he loved her more than words can say. He had
never loved anyone before because no one had asked him, and it wasn't
really the sort of thing he could bring himself to ask. But to repeat, once
given permission, he was the most ardent lover imaginable. He looked up
to her as to something divine, something inconceivably good and beau-
tiful. He could not imagine a more perfect being. She was as providence
itself to him.

He had not bothered much about the fact that she had a little money,
because he didn't understand much about that kind of thing. He used it so
seldom. But of course it was very nice, seeing that everyone talked about
it. He himself felt a kind of reverence at the thought of these things. It
made everything even more wonderful, if possible.

As long as it didn't mean that he would no longer be able to stand
down by the level-crossing gate, because he would certainly miss that. He
was used to it, and once one has gotten used to something, it's hard to go
without. That was his profession, as it were. But if Frida thought it was
beneath him to go on working he would just have to put up with it. It
would probably be all right, even so. That was something he had not liked
to ask her about in so many words. Time enough for that. He loved her,
that was the main thing; he loved her more than he could say, and there
was nothing he wouldn't do for her. He loved Frida for her own sake, and
because it was she who had been good enough to bother about him.

That's how it was. It amounted to love on both sides.

Jonas, yes.... She thought of him, and the kind of man he was.
Thought of when he had thrown his arms around her out in the woods last
spring, and said that she was his most beautiful flower. He could indeed say
so much that was remarkable, things that no one else could have thought
of. He had great gifts, that was certain, which no one but she knew any-
thing about.

Agnes stopped combing.

"There now, Frida, we won't do better than that," she said.

"Oh, my dear, it's lovely! Thank you so much."

They looked at the hair from all angles, and found that it now sat
much better and as prettily as they could wish.

"Now I think we ought to hurry up and get your dress on."

"Yes, I suppose it's nearly time.... Oh, Agnes dear, you've no idea how
strange it feels."

"Yes, it must."

"Just imagine being dressed as a bride—it's all like a dream. I can't really believe it's true."

"If I might suggest it," Agnes said, "you ought to wear your nice black dress instead, it suits you so well."

"Agnes dear, how can you! You're not serious!" Frida looked at her in amazement, quite distressed that she could say anything so thoughtless. "A bride must have white, you know that; it's an occasion for joy."

"Yes, yes, I only meant—that's my opinion—but of course you must do just as you like."

So Frida had her way. It would have been strange if she hadn't, after getting herself the dress for this very moment, sitting up sewing it night after night. And all the dreams she had put into it. Agnes helped her put it on. It was all so beautifully ironed and mustn't be creased at all, and all the lace had to hang properly. But the petticoat was showing at the back. What were they to do—they would have to pin it up.

Agnes stopped to listen.

"The pastor must have come."

"Oh, it's not possible," Frida said softly, feeling herself grow pale.

"You can hear he has, no one's saying a word."

"Then we must get ready," Frida said very quietly. Jonas knocked gently on the half-open door.

"The pastor has come," he whispered reverently.

"Jonas dear, is that you? You can't see me, not yet. In just half a minute, we're just fastening this up. The pastor is here, you said. The time has come then—fancy its hanging down like that—it's funny, isn't it? Dear Agnes, do try and hurry."

"Well, stand still then, so that I can get at it!"

"Yes, yes, of course I will.... what did the pastor say, Jonas?"

"The pastor—what did he say? Oh, he didn't say anything."

"Didn't you say how do you do to him?"

"No, I left the room when he arrived."

"Did you?"

"Yes, I thought I would come up here."

"Yes, it was good of you to come and tell me. Now I'll just put the coronet on, then I'm ready. Jonas dear, are you sure everything is as it should be down there?"

"Yes, Frida dearest, I think everything's all right; it all looks so nice."

"Are the flowerpots in the right place?"

"Yes."

"And the lace cloths on the stools—Hulda won't have forgotten them?"

"No, they're there."

"And the cake? The cake, Jonas! Do you know definitely if it has come?"

"Well, I can't say for sure, but I did see Klas arrive with a cake box; I should think that was probably it."

"Yes, that must have been it. Oh, I hope everything will be all right, and just as it should be, on this great and wonderful day in our life. They did get something to eat with their coffee, Jonas?"

"Yes, indeed."

"You did ask them to help themselves?"

"There was no need, Frida dear."

"Now I think you're ready," Agnes said, giving her a final critical look of inspection.

"Am I! Oh, thank you, Agnes dear. You can come in now, Jonas dear, there's no need for you to go on standing there behind the door."

So Jonas came in. He stood dumbfounded with admiration at this radiant vision in the middle of the room, dazzlingly white and lovely; at his own darling Frida, the sight of whom filled him with an almost dizzy joy. He looked and looked at her with shining eyes, unable to believe it was true.

"Am I all right, dear?"

"Yes," he said, his voice thick and his eyes filling with tears, poor fellow. He couldn't say any more, just pressed and pressed her hand as though to thank her—over and over again.

"Then everything's all right," Frida whispered with a sob. "We can go down together." And she dried her eyes, holding her handkerchief in front of them so as not to show her emotion and how touched she was.

"The bridal bouquet!" cried Agnes, getting it out of the vase and drying it on a towel. It was of pink carnations and greenery.

"Oh, dear Agnes, thank you so much. Fancy forgetting! One forgets everything at a time like this."

And so down they went. Side by side, tightly pressed against each other. The coronet slipped a little to one side going down the stairs, but otherwise all was well. Their eyes were shining as they entered the bridal room, the little room with the sun shining in through the curtains. As they

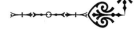

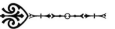

advanced between the guests, the women stared hard at them and the men cleared their throats. Up by the stools the pastor was waiting for them, severe and dignified. They stood in front of him like simple-hearted children, full of devout expectancy. He eyed them over his pince-nez, then opened the book and began to read.

"In the name of God the Father, the Son, and the Holy Ghost...."

They hung on his words. There could not have been two more attentive listeners, so afraid were they of missing a single word, so moved by the solemnity of the moment. Jonas did indeed smile as usual, but it was merely out of inexpressible reverence. He kept his head a little on one side in order to hear everything, and his hands were clasped together in implicit reliance on what was being said to him. Frida, too, held her hands tightly together with the bouquet between them, and looked at the pastor with trusting, humble gratitude.

Presently, when they had to kneel down, they thought that was the loveliest of all. The sun shone on them, on Frida's lovely white dress with the veil all around it that seemed to be made of light, and on Jonas in his brand-new clothes. They were kneeling right in front of the window, and so their eyes shone with an almost supernatural radiance. Around them were all the flowerpots. It was a moment full of light and beauty.

The others, of course, could not feel it in the same way. They were only there because they were invited. But God's word was being read out, so of course it was a solemn occasion. The women were a little weepy, as they always are at weddings, and everyone listened to the trembling voices

answering the time-honored questions. It was certainly nice being there when they knew Jonas very well, too.

The pastor gave no address for them, nor was there any need for one. But he read Our Father and the Benediction, and they thought it had never sounded so beautiful; they were like two completely new prayers with memorable new words that applied only to them. Then he closed the book, and the moving ceremony was at an end. Frida and Jonas were wedded to each other for always.

Wine was handed around and everyone drank with them; first the pastor, who wished them happiness, then all the others according to age and position or relationship. The sun shone on the glasses, they clinked and sparkled all at once, the entire little room had something so festive about it. In the middle of the guests, entirely surrounded, stood the bride, radiant with happiness. And beside her stood Jonas, smiling with every wrinkle of his kind face. They drank to him, too, and he held his glass extended between his fingertips as though he were holding out an extraordinary kind of flower. Everywhere were kindly eyes that must be thanked, and he kept bowing incessantly. A wave of warmth and cordiality flowed toward him such as he could never have imagined. Then it grew a little quieter; they all sat down at the window tables or over on the sofa and began talking among themselves, and he was left to himself in the middle of the floor, quite a lot to himself.

But the women took hold of Frida by the arm to say a few words more heartfelt than the mere congratulations.

"Well, Frida dear, now you have got what you wanted, so I suppose you are happy, aren't you?"

"Oh yes, thank you, Mrs. Lundgren, I am indeed. I am as happy as it is possible for anyone to be."

"Yes, I suppose you are, Frida dear."

And all the relatives had to go up and talk to her for a moment.

"So you're married, Frida dear."

"Yes, Emma dear."

"Oh well, you never know how things will turn out."

"Yes, who would have thought it would be like this? But then we don't really know what's ahead of us."

"Oh," put in Miss Svensson from the tobacconist's, "I always thought that Frida would get married. I said many times that it's a wonder Frida Johansson doesn't get married. She easily could."

"Yes, that's just what I thought. My old man always used to say as we sat talking about the family, 'No, Frida will never get married.' But I thought, no, it's always best to wait and see, one never really knows for sure. Well, good luck, Frida dear, we are all so glad that you've managed it."

"Thank you, thank you, dear Matilda.

So the talk went on, Frida smiling and happy. After all, she had Jonas. They nodded at each other secretively, their gaze still obscured, the sacred words resounding within them. They were now a little apart from each other, but that didn't matter, it was only for a little while. And it was all going so well—she could see he thought so, too. Oh yes, everyone was so nice and kind. Some of them had come a long way in order to be present on this, their great day. Strange that there were so many gathered here just for their sake. There were so many conversations going on that it was hard to follow them, and one didn't know whom to listen to. And just think how festive it was when they had all come up and drunk their health.

Now there was the smell of cooking from the kitchen, and the women began wondering what it was they were going to have; it was sure to be roast meat, as was customary. Frida was sure to have only the best, and she could no doubt afford it. What her income was from the little shop no one could say. And Hulda was going to do the waiting, ah yes. And she had a lace apron, well I never.

The pastor came up and said he must be going. There was nothing much to wait for at a wedding like this, and he had so much work to do at home, routine office work as it is called. No, of course he didn't know who Frida was, and what she had to offer. How should he know?

Frida had hoped that he would stay. He is sure to, she had thought. It would make it all so festive. But he was obliged to go. Yes, of course, when he had such an awful lot to do; one can imagine a clergyman who is responsible for all that is most important in life, for the souls of so many people. Yes, there must be a lot of work, a lot that is not apparent. She thanked him for making this moment so sacred, for all the beautiful words he had read. Both she and Jonas went to the door with him, and Jonas helped him on with his coat and opened the gate leading out into the road, where he stood bowing until the pastor had disappeared through the trees.

Dinner was ready now, and they all sat down, the bridal pair in the principal seats in the center of one side, and the others gathered around them for this banquet in honor of the newly married. The men were

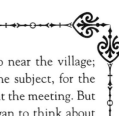

talking of a sewer which emptied out into the lake too near the village; they had been discussing it and were going to finish the subject, for the farmers didn't know what a fuss there had been about it at the meeting. But now they got their smörgåsbord and an aquavit and began to think about eating. There was plenty to choose from, dishes of every kind, and there was nothing wrong with the aquavit either, so they had another. They began to feel nice and cheery, as was fitting at a wedding. Now that old Frida was getting married, they must see that it was done properly, and eat and drink as much as they could when it was offered once in a while.

"Come on, Jonas, have a stiffener, it won't hurt you."

"What, isn't he drinking?" shouted Emil of Östragård, Frida's second cousin, across the table. "I should think he needs one! Go on, have one, it'll put a tongue in your head."

And Jonas smiled and took it, though he didn't usually touch that kind of thing, but of course he must when they wanted him to join them.

"Well, to think it's come to a wedding. Who would have thought it!"

"Oh, more surprising things than this can happen. Sometimes they're in such a hurry that it makes you wonder what's wrong. No question of that in this case!"

"No, Julius, that it isn't! Cheers! You were always a wag!"

"No, by Christ, if they want to swap bullocks with me, then they'll have to bring along the best they have and still pay the difference. I told him so, too. No, it was the most rotten cattle market I've ever been to."

"Didn't you even get a drink?"

"No, the place was shut."

"Oh well, then, of course you couldn't do any business."

"Hey there, Emil, fill them up here! You can't keep it all down on your end!"

They went on drinking after the roast beef was brought in, and Jonas had to join in, though he didn't want to. "You're a damn queer sort of chap, not drinking." He was to have a drop in him, same as they. So Jonas drank, though he tried to have as little as possible. He was one of those people who just couldn't say no. And they all meant so well, wanting him to join in.

"Take a stiff one and get your strength up; you've got a good day's work ahead of you such as you never did in your life before, I'll bet!"

"You must at least have a good strong breath if Frida's to be satisfied with you."

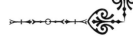

"Well, you're in for a good time now, Jonas. No need for you to go and overwork in any way."

"Are you going to give up your job at the hotel? Oh, you don't know. Hasn't she said anything yet?"

"Perhaps you'll be selling embroidery in your old age. Well, not so bad either, a nice dainty job. And I suppose you'll have to go poking about here with all these flowers. Frida's got a frightful lot of flowerpots, that she has."

"What's the idea; is Jonas going to help in your shop, or what are you going to make him do?"

There was no need for Frida to answer; they were all talking at once and there was a terrific hubbub. She sat looking straight in front of her with her big, gentle eyes, the bridal coronet slightly askew, but dignified and calm in her white dress, which really suited her very well when you came to think of it. Now and then she would squeeze Jonas's hand under the table, and she would light up with a blissful smile as they looked at each other with secret joy. Then she would grow serious again, almost melancholy.

It was twilight now, and Hulda had to light the lamps. The sweet was brought in. It had turned out very well, but Frida could not eat much; she just tasted it to see that it was all right. Yes, of course, it was all right; they'd taken such trouble with it. And then came the cake. IT was certainly very handsome. In the middle was a J and an F in bright red jam, but no one noticed it, and besides the letters were all intertwined. But she and Jonas saw it, and they gave each other a happy, tender look, and held each other's hand under the table. Wine was served with the cake. If the pastor had been able to stay he would probably have made a speech for them now, he would indeed. He could make a very good speech when he had to. But it all went very well notwithstanding and the cake was eaten up.

Afterwards there was to be coffee. They all got up from the table and spread out over the room, the men talking and booming, a little unsteady on their feet. Cigars were handed around and the coffee was poured out.

"Haven't you any brandy, Frida?" asked Emil.

No, that's something she had forgotten. It hadn't really occurred to her that they would drink so much on an occasion like this.

"Well, that's stingy when we're celebrating like this," Emil said. "It is a wedding, you know, so there ought to be some brandy, see! I've got a bottle out in the trap that I went and bought, so we can have that." And he lumbered out through the door, returning in a minute with the bottle.

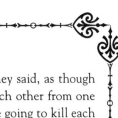

"Now for a drop in the coffee!"

They started drinking. They shouted everything they said, as though they were standing out in the fields yelling across at each other from one farm to the next, and they all swore as though they were going to kill each other when they met, though they were firm friends standing close together, all talking at once. They became more and more drunk as the evening wore on, swaying against each other and sitting down heavily so that the chairs creaked. The ones from the village were a little more dignified—they had grown rather more superior—but those farmers were really too awful. The room was filled with fumes from the liquor and the warm smell of billowing smoke.

The women were having a nice time on their own. They had gathered in one corner and were talking about people who were not there, and what had happened in the district—there was quite a lot since last time, for there were not so many parties nowadays. Then they spoke their minds, shaking their heads, pursing their lips, whispering and listening and repeating things, whatever it happened to be. Frida sat with them for a while, then cast an eye into the kitchen, rearranged the flowers that had not been put back as they should, and saw to the lamp. Finally she just stood in the middle of the floor with her hands clasped, looking in front of her and listening to the noise all around her.

"Silly little thing, decking herself out in white," she heard someone say behind her. Then she went over and sat by Jonas, and as she sat down she burst into tears.

But she wasn't really crying, the tears ran so gently and quietly down her cheeks. No one noticed them except Jonas. He got really frightened; he patted her and took her hand, holding it tenderly in his, asking over and over again what was wrong and why she was crying. Then she looked at him so warmly and smiled so sweetly, as she always did when they spoke to each other.

"It's nothing, Jonas dear, it's only tears of joy."

Then he was reassured, because he could see that it was true.

"Dear Jonas," she said then, "We'll go upstairs now."

And so they did. They said good-bye to everybody, happily and affectionately, like the bridal pair they were, and went up to their room.

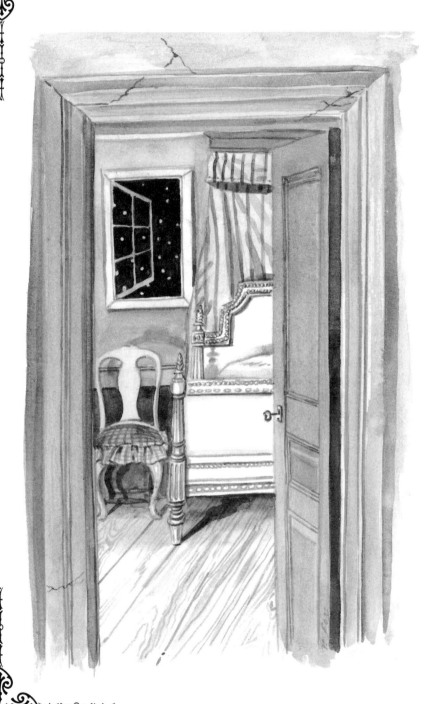

It had all been set up just as Frida had planned—the bed was prepared nicely with sheets with lace insertions (the widest in the shop); there were freshly cut flowers on the table, a clean white cloth with hemstitching, and the same on the chest of drawers. The window was open to the silence of the late summer night with its stars shining in.

How quiet and peaceful it was here. They threw their arms around each other, overwhelmed with bliss. They stood there, full of their happiness, for a long while, so long that they lost track of time. Downstairs the noise continued, but, strangely, they did not hear it. It was strange not hearing a single thing, not one thing at all.

They undressed and got into bed, caressing and whispering to each other. They felt the most wonderful feeling, a feeling they had never known, which was like nothing else—nothing.

She had never thought that love could be so great. She had thought a lot about all this, but had never really been able to imagine it. It was as though she had lived her life just for this moment she and Jonas became one. He held her in his arms, strong from all he had carried in his life, and she gave herself to her beloved; it was so unspeakably lovely to give him all she had, so really wonderful. She bit him with her false teeth so hard he became dizzy. She, too, felt a little stupefied afterwards, but it was love speaking, that great, divine love, the incomprehensible miracle which made everything sacred.

Then they lay side by side, tired and blissful, holding each other's hand, as though that were even more tender than being caressed. They were almost numbed by the perfection of their happiness.

Jonas fell asleep, replete with the day's events. He was so handsome and good as he lay there beside her on the pillow; she stroked his hair and arranged it. She, too, felt a little exhausted, but lay listening in the semidarkness with open eyes.

How quiet it was, how exceptionally quiet. Were they still there, or had they gone? She heard nothing but the great unfathomable night, and the loved one at her side snoring softly. Otherwise, there was nothing.

She crept down beside him and she, too, fell asleep, his hand tightly clasped in hers. They lay together in the darkness, close together with burning cheeks and mouths half-open for a kiss. And like a heavenly song of praise, like a hosanna of light around the only living thing, the stars rose around their bed in mighty hosts, their numbers increasing with the darkness.

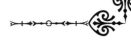

Short Stories

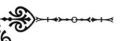

The Wedding Night

Unnur Benediktsdóttir

The church bells were ringing.

Their sound, as bright and cheerful a sound possible from an old set of bells, carried into the houses. Everyone smiled. Some went to the window or door and looked out. The prettiest girl in town was to be married that night. The young girls were all donning their best—they were going to the wedding. Servants rushed back and forth through the houses, constantly in search of some necessary article. At last, dressed in all their finery, the girls came down to the parlor to mothers and grandmothers and, happy and carefree, left for the church. The older women shook their heads after the girls had departed. Yes, indeed, they knew life. Marriage could be a failure even though the bride was as lovely as a day in spring and the groom a fine fellow.

It was a bright July evening, the sky blue and gold. As the village clock struck six, the bridal procession filed through the streets.

On the slope to the west of the village lay the cemetery, affording a fine view over the buildings and the fjord beyond. By a grave on which the grass was beginning to sprout a young man sat and watched the procession until it disappeared within the church, far in the south end of town. Long after the church doors had closed, he stood gazing at them.

Then, turning around, he looked down at the grave and softly sighed.

He had had but one intimate friend, and that friend now rested there under the sod. He had loved but one woman, and now she knelt before the altar at another's side.

Though the sun warmed his neck and cheek, he was unaware of it. Though the fragrance of the birches from the glen was wafted to him by a soft breeze, he did not feel it. He was communing with his friend: "To you alone I could have told it. Only you knew it all."

He bent his head down upon the grass. It cooled his fevered brow, though the soil was parched by the sun. Perhaps it was mere fancy, but his thoughts seemed the calmer for it. He lay still, watching the procession of visions from bygone days.

In each one of them she appeared.

First as a light-footed little girl, in a short red dress, and straw hat that would never stay on her head, but fell down on her back where, held by

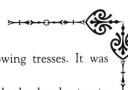

elastic, it bobbed up and down on her loosely flowing tresses. It was delightful to see her run and hear her laugh.

Then, a little older, she flashed by on a sled with cheeks glowing in the cold.

Next he saw her walking serenely, clad in her confirmation dress, the loveliest among her companions. She had waited at the gate that day and looked in his direction as he passed by with his friend. He hardly dared to extend congratulations; she seemed so grown-up, almost a bride.

Then one night at a dance she had flown with him straight into a heaven of bliss. With her alone was happiness; all else was sadness. Later he learned the reason for her high spirits and her gaiety: she had just learned that her dearest hope was to come true. Thinking back, he remembered that she had been equally gay with everyone. He had thought her smiles were meant for him alone.

Now a shadow darkened his reverie.

He was following his friend to the last resting place and she disappeared for a moment. Upon return, she was no longer alone. A handsome young man walked at her side.

Last of all came the vision in the bridal veil. He looked searchingly into her eyes. "Don't you remember? Don't you remember? No one has loved you more than I." Her hair was spread out beneath the bridal veil; her lips were red; her arms lovelier than ever. She gave him a friendly smile and passed on. He could see the broad shoulders of the bridegroom at her side.

His sorrow crept into every nerve. As he faced future without her, the cold and darkness gripped him like a midday eclipse.

Once again the church bells pealed.

He rose to his feet and saw her come out of the church, white as a cloud in the summer sky, her husband like a shadow at her side. Slowly they approached. Now they were passing the cemetery. He could see the flowers in her bridal veil and her profile standing out above the grating in the gate. No one in the bridal party saw him. He was glad. No one must know where he was. No one must divine his thoughts. The procession was very long. Now and again the bride would disappear to the rear among the guests, but she always returned, looking white and as pure as a dove. Everything seemed so strangely dark in contrast. Then she crossed the threshold of the man she loved, and disappeared, never to return.

In his mind's eye he could see a picture of her the next morning coming outside, lovely with the dignity of a wife, while he, poor unfortunate beggar, would stand far away.

Once again the future opened before him, a vast pitch dark expanse, without sun or stars. The darkness was weighted down upon his shoulders. He hid his face in the grave and wept.

The evening was nearly spent. Worn with violent weeping, he shivered in the chilly air. He leaned against the grave. The stones cast their black shadows behind them, while out beyond the shore stretched the dark blue sea. The dew began to fall, softly, very softly. On the hill a plover still sang; it tripped along, faltering, then sang so beautifully, its breast gleaming in the last rays of the setting sun. A gentle breeze ran along the ground, stirring every flower and every blade of grass as though seeking to discover whether they had actually dropped off into sleep. Then it passed, leaving a dead calm.

The eastern sky was bright, giving promise of a fine day. The blue haze which veiled everything in the east would later lift, and the first rays of light would appear. Then dawn would come, lighting up the clouds with brilliant hues, and at last the sun itself would rise.

The young man in the cemetery stood up. He looked to the west, where the sun had set; he ran his eyes to the north, out to sea; finally he brought them to rest on the blue of the eastern sky. In that soft, dark hue his spirit found peace. He was exhausted by his combat with reality which had held him so tightly that he could not hear the voice of his own heart.

Little did he realize that his thoughts were like the blue of the summer sky just before daybreak, which changes first to the brilliant hues of dawn, then gives way to a clear, bright day.

from The Bride Comes to Yellow Sky

STEPHEN CRANE

Potter and his bride walked sheepishly and with speed. Sometimes they laughed together shamefacedly and low.

"Next corner, dear," he said finally.

They put forth the efforts of a pair walking bowed against a strong wind. Potter was about to raise a finger to point out the first appearance of the new home when, as they circled the corner, they came face to face with a man in a maroon-colored shirt, who was feverishly pushing cartridges into a large revolver. Upon the instant the man dropped his revolver to the ground and, like lightning, whipped another from its holster. The second weapon was aimed at the bridegroom's chest.

SHORT STORIES

There was a silence. Potter's mouth seemed to be merely a grave for his tongue. He exhibited an instinct to at once loosen his arm from the woman's grip, and he dropped the bag to the sand. As for the bride, her face had gone as yellow as old cloth. She was a slave to hideous rites, gazing at the apparitional snake.

The two men faced each other at a distance of three paces. He of the revolver smiled with a new and quiet ferocity.

"Tried to sneak up on me," he said. "Tried to sneak up on me!" His eyes grew more baleful. As Potter made a slight movement, the man thrust his revolver venomously forward. "No; don't you do it, Jack Potter. Don't you move a finger toward a gun just yet. Don't you move an eyelash. The time has come for me to settle with you, and I'm goin' to do it my own way, and loaf along with no interferin'. So if you don't want a gun bent on you, just mind what I tell you."

Potter looked at his enemy. "I ain't got a gun on me, Scratchy," he said. "Honest, I ain't." He was stiffening and steadying, but yet somewhere at the back of his mind a vision of the Pullman floated: the sea-green figured velvet, the shining brass, silver, and glass, the wood that gleamed as darkly brilliant as the surface of a pool of oil—all the glory of the marriage, the environment of the new estate. "You know I fight when it comes to sighting, Scratchy Wilson, but I ain't got a gun on me. You'll have to do all the shootin' yourself."

His enemy's face went livid. He stepped forward, and lashed his weapon to and fro before Potter's chest. "Don't you tell me you ain't got no gun on you, you whelp. Don't tell me no lie like that. There ain't a man in Texas ever seen you without no gun. Don't take me for no kid." His eyes blazed with light, and his throat worked like a pump.

"I ain't takin' you for no kid," answered Potter. His heels had not moved an inch backward. "I'm takin' you for a damn fool. I tell you I ain't got a gun, and I ain't. If you're goin' to shoot me up, you better begin now; you'll never get a chance like this again."

So much enforced reasoning had told on Wilson's rage; he was calmer. "If you ain't got a gun, why ain't you got a gun?" he sneered. "Been to Sunday-school?"

"I ain't got a gun because I've just come from San Anton' with my wife. I'm married," said Potter. "And if I'd thought there was going to be any galoots like you prowling around when I brought my wife home, I'd had a gun, and don't you forget it."

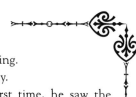

"Married!" said Scratchy, not at all comprehending.

"Yes, married. I'm married," said Potter, distinctly.

"Married?" said Scratchy. Seemingly for the first time, he saw the drooping, drowning woman at the other man's side. "No!" he said. He was like a creature allowed a glimpse of another world. He moved a pace backward, and his arm, with the revolver, dropped to his side. "Is this the lady?" he asked.

"Yes; this is the lady," answered Potter.

There was another period of silence.

"Well," said Wilson at last, slowly, "I s'pose it's all off now."

"It's all off if you say so, Scratchy. You know I didn't make the trouble." Potter lifted his valise.

"Well, I 'low it's off, Jack," said Wilson. He was looking at the ground. "Married!" He was not a student of chivalry; it was merely that in the presence of this foreign condition he was a simple child of the earlier plains. He picked up his starboard revolver, and, placing both weapons in their holsters, he went away. His feet made funnel-shaped tracks in the heavy sand.

Marriage in Moderation

John Erksine

They were friends of mine, and I tried to improve on their happiness!
He was a writer, a novelist if you must know all, and she painted land-
scapes.

She came to Eighth Street first—he, several weeks after, but fate intro-
duced them properly. The great days of the Village were already a legend.
That was how they had heard of it, he in Altoona, she in Baltimore. They
had read of freedom of plain lodgings, two flights up, with a flower box in the
window and no running water. She found such a haven at once, he rested
cautiously at a small hotel until he got his bearings and found her.

From their reading they both knew you couldn't be free if you were
alone. Freedom meant a soul mate, which meant a roommate. But nothing
vulgar. No marriage.

Freedom was at its peak when you took your courage in your hand and
tacked two calling cards on your door, "Mr. So-and-so," and "Miss This-
and-that"—sometimes the girl's name on top and sometimes the man's, but
either way you were conscious of independence when you opened the door
in the morning to take in the milk, and remembered that the landlady had
her thoughts about such things.

I'll call them Wallace and Belle. When I made their acquaintance
they had been free for a year, and if they had not outlined their true con-
dition with aggressive frankness I should have taken them for man and
wife, signed and sealed, in the sober tradition of Victoria the Queen. Never
have I laid eyes on a pair so fitted for domestic propriety, companionship
and trust. They had the fiber of constancy in them, that friendly warp and
woof which knits the home all of a piece, from the first sunshiny spinning
of the threads to the shadowy trimming of the pattern at the end.

I frequented their simple but blessed hearth just to look on marriage in
its essential perfection, and it annoyed me when they announced again, as
they always did before the evening was over, that they weren't married at all.

"You might as well be!" I protested at last. "It's permanent. Why
pretend?"

Belle brushed back her lovely, tousled hair so that her honest blue eyes
could get at me.

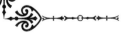

"We have the reality. Should we walk up an aisle—and all that flumdiddle?"

"The city hall would do," I conceded.

Here Wallace got on his long legs, remarked that my pipe had gone out, and offered fresh tobacco, so I took the hint and said no more.

But when I called again, off they went on that freedom theme of theirs, and now I had a better argument ready.

"It's a pity you two don't believe in self-expression. If you did, you'd be great artists!"

That stirred them, as I knew it would.

"No," I persisted, "if you believed in expression, you'd marry. You'd do it with the full flumdiddle. An emotion is stronger, an idea is clearer, for being expressed. In true art there can't be any hiding. This unadmitted wedlock of yours—well, it isn't art."

When I left that night, I thought I had merely spoiled the evening, but the next afternoon Wallace called up to say that they had been to the city hall, and I was right! You couldn't realize what marriage was like till you gave it public expression.

I had them to dinner at the Cafe de Paris, and they talked of nothing but their new discovery that vows are satisfying, provided you mean them. They were, if I may say so, daffy with romance, and the cafe put Europe in their head.

They decided then and there to take an old-fashioned wedding trip.

Where they got the money I don't know. Perhaps the relatives in Altoona and Baltimore made a thank offering. Anyway, they went to England, and I stood on the dock and waved up at them, conscious of a good job.

A month later I had to go over myself, and I ran into them in Paris. He was halfway through a new book, which she said was inspired, and he didn't argue. She had bought paint and canvas, and was doing an entirely original view of Notre Dame from the river bank.

Also, they had made up their minds to be married in the historic church, and I was to be a witness.

"It's so much more beautiful than the city hall," explained Belle. "It will express our love!"

"You aren't Catholics, are you?" I asked, knowing their indifference to details.

"That can be arranged," said Wallace earnestly, "Or if necessary we can join the church."

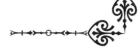

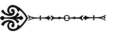

It took time, but somehow it was indeed arranged, and I looked on with the concierge's wife, and then I gave them a dinner at La Perousse.

We were just uncorking a bottle of Montrachet, when Wallace remarked casually, "I felt it far more deeply this time than at St. Margaret's, in London. The architecture's nobler."

Belle glowed with beatitude. "Or our love has grown!"

My hand shook—I couldn't lift my glass.

"What did you two do at St. Margaret's?" I asked.

"Got married," said Belle. "The most charming old curate with white hair, and that placid little church, right under the abbey—"

"Did you tell him you were already married?"

"Only a civil ceremony," said Wallace, disposing of me. "Belle, have you tried this spinach? It has cheese on it, and mushrooms."

"Wait a minute!" said I. "Did the French priest know you were married in London?"

"None of his business," said Wallace. "Can't I marry my own wife? If marriage is, as you said, a form of expression, then the more you feel married, the more you ought to express it. Belle and I are happier every day. Aren't we, darling?"

They really were, so I get it lie, and in a week they vanished from Paris, leaving a trail of bliss.

I heard nothing more till I got his telegram.

When they reached Chartres they discovered that the Cathedral was finer than Notre Dame by precisely the proportion that their love meanwhile had matured.

They were moved to express themselves again, and did the necessary registering at the Hotel de Ville, where the clerks are trained to check up on you.

To a marriage in England the French may pay no attention, but to a marriage in France they do.

Wallace's telegram read: "Come down and bail us out. We're arrested for bigamy."

When I got there the charge had been shifted to insanity and Wallace and Belle were quarreling.

I hate to see a husband and wife exchanging words, like two dogs tied together.

Wallace and Belle are living in New York now—they're still married.

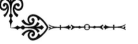

Wedding Breakfast

Elizabeth Head Fetter

There was to be a wedding in the afternoon, the wedding of a very close friend, so I came down to breakfast that morning feeling somewhat dewy.

"I told her," I said gently, "that with all the noise of the caterers and florists at their apartment, she must just come here and rest until time for the wedding. I think I'll give her lunch and then read her to sleep. Wouldn't you?"

Jonas said he should think she would have too much to do to waste her wedding day being read to.

"That's just it," I explained patiently. "She must get away from it all. She must leave all the last-minute fuss for someone else and just relax. She'll probably want to cry. I did, I remember. I cried for about an hour."

"Did you?" asked Jonas.

"Yes," I said, "I did, and she rubbed my head with cologne and told me how nice you were and how much I was going to like you."

"I remember now," said Jonas, his voice getting dreamy. "You were away all that day, weren't you? I remember wishing at lunch time that you were there. We had the most marvelous lunch; mutton chops grilled on pineapple and topped with bacon, and asparagus with Hollandaise, and I think strawberries."

"I don't remember what I had for lunch that day," I said. "I don't believe I ate any."

"Oh, yes, you did," said Jonas, his memory still holding, "because after the ceremony, Susie was telling me about it. She said the reason you looked so lovely and rested was that you had had a nice lunch and nap. You had creamed sweetbreads and orange Charlotte. I remember because when she told me, I thought how much better ours had been and that you really should have stayed home."

"That was sweet of you," I said. "As a matter of fact, I never looked worse in my life. I looked like an old woman. I remember thinking when I put on my veil that it was a good thing I was wearing one."

"Darling, you looked lovely," said Jonas. I felt he was finally getting the wedding spirit. I reached over and gently patted his hand.

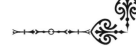

SHORT STORIES

"I remember it all perfectly," he went on. "You looked so calm and sort of hay. I remember thinking how glad I was you weren't one of those languishing brides, and how I wanted to laugh when you started on your second lobster cutlet."

A Wife can stand just so much misrepresentation. "Jonas, you're absolutely crazy," I said. "I hardly touched my cutlet. I know because I remember thinking what a shame it was I couldn't eat, because I probably wouldn't have lobster very often in the future."

"But you were wrong, weren't you?" said Jonas smugly. "You've had it any number of times. Think of Cape Cod last summer. You had three that time."

I could see things were rapidly getting out of control.

"You're such a gourmet, dear," I said sweetly. "You'll have to help me. What would be nice to give Susie for lunch? Something light, you know, but tempting."

"Why don't you give her mutton chops grilled on pineapple?" said Jonas. "They're tempting enough. I don't believe I've had one since the wedding." There was a light in his eye I hadn't seen for a long time.

"I'll tell you what," he went on. "You have mutton chops on pineapple, and I'll leave the office early and come home for lunch. Then I can help you amuse Susie till it's time for her to dress. That will be much better than reading. Reading would probably give her the jitters. What do you say?"

"I'm afraid mutton chops would be a trifle heavy," I said, gazing out the window over his shoulder. "I think I'll have creamed sweetbreads and orange Charlotte. That won't be quite enough lunch for you, will it, dear?"

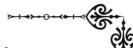

The Wedding March

SELMA LAGERLÖF

Now I will relate to you a nice story.

A good many years ago there was to be a very big wedding at Svartsjö parish in Vermland.

First, there was to be a church ceremony, then after that three days of feasting and merrymaking, and every day while the festivities went on there was to be dancing from early morning till far into the night.

Since there was to be so much dancing, it was of very great importance to have a good fiddler, and councilor Nils Olafsson, who was managing the wedding, worried more over this than over almost anything else.

He did not care to engage the fiddler at Svartsjö whose name was Jan Oster. To be sure, the councilor knew that he was well-known, but he was so poor that sometimes he would appear at a wedding in a frayed jacket and no shoes. The councilor didn't wish to see such a bum at the head of the bridal procession so he decided to send a messenger to a musician in Jösse parish, who was commonly called Fiddler Mårten, and ask him if he would come and play at the wedding.

Fiddler Mårten didn't consider the proposition for a moment, but promptly replied that he did not want to play at Svartsjö because a musician who was more skilled than all others in Vermland lived there. As long as they had him, there was no need for them to call another.

When Nils Olafsson received this answer, he took a few days to think it over, then sent word to a fiddler in Big Kil parish, Olle of Säby, to ask him if he would come to play at his daughter's wedding.

Olle of Säby answered in the same way as Fiddler Mårten. He sent his compliments to Nils Olafsson, and said that so long as there was such a capable musician as Jan Oster to be found in Svartsjö, he didn't want to go there to play.

Nils Olafsson didn't like it that the musicians tried in this way to force upon him the very one he did not want. Now he considered that it was a point of honor for him to get a fiddler other than Jan Oster.

A few days after he received the answer from Olle of Säby, he sent his servant to fiddler Lars Larsson, who lived at the game lodge in Ullerud parish. Lars Larsson was a well-to-do man who owned a fine farm. He was

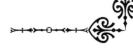

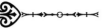

sensible and considerate and no hotspur, like the other musicians. But Lars Larsson, like the others, at once thought of Jan Oster, and asked how it happened that he was not to play at the wedding.

Nils Olafsson's servant thought it best to say to him that, since Jan Oster lived at Svartsjö, they could hear him play at any time. As Nils Olafsson was making ready to give a grand wedding, he wished to treat his guests to something a little better and more select.

"I doubt if you can get anyone better," said Lars Larsson.

"Now you must be thinking of answering in the same way as fiddler Mårten and Olle in Säby did," said the servant. Then he told him how he had fared with them.

Lars Larsson paid close attention to the servant's story, and then he sat quietly for a long while and pondered. Finally he answered in the affirmative: "Tell your master that I thank him for his invitation and will come."

The following Sunday Lars Larsson journeyed down to Svartsjö. He drove up to the church knoll just as the wedding guests were forming a line to march into the church. He came driving in his own chaise with a good horse and dressed in black broadcloth. He took out his fiddle from a highly polished box. Nils Olafsson received him effusively, thinking that here was a fiddler of whom he might be proud.

Immediately after Lars Larsson's arrival, Jan Oster, too, came marching up to the church, with his fiddle under his arm. He walked straight up to the crowd around the bride, exactly as if he were asked to come and play at the wedding.

Jan Oster had come in the old gray homespun jacket which they had seen him wearing for ages. But, as this was to be such a grand wedding, his wife had made an attempt to mend the holes at the elbow by sewing big green patches over them. Jan Oster was a tall handsome man, and would have made a fine appearance at the head of the bridal procession, had he not been so shabbily dressed, and had his face not been so lined and seamed by worries and struggles with misfortune.

When Lars Larsson saw Jan Oster coming, he seemed a bit displeased. "So you called Jan Oster, too," he said under his breath to Councilor Nils Olafsson, "but at a grand wedding there's no harm in having two fiddlers."

"I didn't invite him, that's for sure!" protested Nils Olafsson. "I can't comprehend why he has come. Just wait, and I'll let him know that he has no business here!"

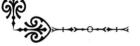

"Then some practical joker must have bidden him," said Lars Larsson. "But if you care to be guided by my counsel, appear as if nothing were wrong and go over and bid him welcome. I heard that he's quick-tempered, and who knows if he'll begin to quarrel if you tell him he wasn't invited?"

The councilor knew this, too! It was no time to begin fussing as the bridal procession was forming on church grounds; so he walked up to Jan Oster and welcomed him. Then the two fiddlers took their places at the head of the procession. The bridal couple walked under a canopy, the bridesmaids and the groomsmen marched in pairs, and after them came the parents and relatives; the procession was long and imposing.

When everything was ready, a groomsman stepped up to the musicians and asked them to play the "Wedding March". Both musicians swung their fiddles up to their chins, but they did not get beyond that. They just stood there. It was an old custom in Svartsjö for the best fiddler to strike up the "Wedding March" and lead the music.

The groomsman looked at Lars Larsson as though he were waiting for him to start; but Lars Larsson looked to Jan Oster and said, "It is you, Jan Oster, who must begin."

It did not seem possible to Jan Oster that the other fiddler, who was as finely dressed as any gentleman, should not be better than himself, who had come in his old homespun jacket straight from the wretched hovel where there was only poverty and distress. "No, indeed!" said he. "No, indeed!"

He saw that the bridegroom put forth his hand and touched Lars Larsson. "Larsson, let's begin," said he.

When Jan Oster heard the bridegroom say this, he promptly lowered his fiddle and stepped aside.

Lars Larsson, on the other hand, did not move from the spot, but remained standing in his place, confident and pleased with himself. Nor did he raise the bow. "It is Jan Oster who must begin," he repeated stubbornly resisting, as one used to having his way.

There was some commotion amongst the crowd over the cause of the delay. The bride's father came forward and begged Lars Larsson to begin. The sexton stepped to the door of the church and beckoned to them to hurry along. The parson stood waiting at the altar.

"You can ask Jan Oster to begin then," said Lars Larsson. "We musicians consider him to be the best among us."

"That may be so," said a peasant, "but we peasants consider you the best one."

SHORT STORIES

Then the other peasants also gathered around them. "Well, begin, why don't you?" they said. "The parson is waiting. We'll become a laughing-stock to the church people."

Lars Larsson stood there quite as stubborn and determined as before. "I can't see why the people in this parish are so opposed to having their own fiddler placed in the lead."

Nils Olafsson was perfectly furious that they wanted to force Jan Oster upon him in that fashion. He leaned close to Lars Larsson and whispered: "I comprehend that it is you who called Jan Oster here, and that you arranged this to do him honor. But be quick now and own up, or I'll drive that ragamuffin from the church grounds in disgrace by force!"

Lars Larsson looked him square in the face and nodded to him without displaying any irritation. "Yes, you are right in saying that we must have an end to this," he said.

He beckoned Jan Oster to return to his place. Then he himself walked forward a step or two, and turned around that all might see him. Then he flung the bow far from him, pulled out his pocket knife and cut all four violin strings, which snapped with a sharp twang. "It shall not be said of me that I count myself better than Jan Oster!" said he.

It appears that for three years Jan Oster had been sweating over a tune that he couldn't get out of the strings because he was so full of dark worries, and nothing ever happened to him, either great or small, to lift him above the daily grind. But when he heard Lars Larsson's strings snap, he threw back his head and filled his lungs. His features were rapt, as though he were listening to something far away, and began to play. The tune that he had been musing over for three years became suddenly clear to him, and as the tones of it vibrated he walked with a proud gait down to the church.

The bridal procession had never before heard a tune like that; it carried them along with such speed that not even Nils Olafsson could think of staying back. And everyone was so pleased with both Jan Oster and Lars Larsson, that the entire procession entered the church, their eyes brimming with tears of joy.

SHORT STORIES

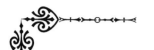

The Wedding

AINO KALLAS

A hundred years ago a wedding was being celebrated on a Saaremaa farm. In the middle of the room sat the bride, so that all might see her heated young face. The cap newly fastened to her hair and which she was still unaccustomed to, compelled her to hold her head well back; otherwise she hardly looked the type to bow her head very much. She kept her hands on her lap over her apron, which had just been patched. The guests filed by with copper and silver coins in their hands and threw these into the apron. She thanked them and laughed—seeming to wait for the opportunity to give rein to the boundless mirth within her. When the money had been put away, one of the guests seized from the ring a boy about five years of age standing around the bride, and set him on her knee for her infant. Jokes and innuendoes rained on her from all sides, grave prophetic hopes and bold quips, sufficient to drive the blood time and again to the bride's cheeks.

Despite the courage and sincerity of her character, confusion finally seized her and she lifted the boy to the floor; she felt hot, the head-dress weighed on her temples, a desire to leave the room awoke in her. Hardly noticed, she drew aside, the cooks at that moment beginning to wipe the tables, striking them with loud knocks to solicit contributions. The violins were being tuned in the corner. She edged closer and closer to the open door and finally slipped through it. In the village lane, where geese waddled with their brown-coated young, she almost broke into a run before reaching the well. No one noticed her disappearance but the bridegroom, who all the time had kept his eyes on her and now set off after her.

He found his newly-wedded wife on the ledge of the well, bowed down in an attempt to hoist the bucket. A fence and a cluster of hop-bushed sheltered them from the house. Hearing footsteps, she turned as though caught in some evil deed. "It was so hot," she said, as though begging for his forgiveness. But the bridegroom stood holding the well's post, unhurriedly gazing at his bride—then, as though by some silent agreement, she sat herself down on the cover of the well, in the cracks of which the grass grew. "Let's stay here awhile," she begged. The bridegroom nodded his head without removing his gaze from her face, and to both came a feeling

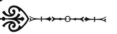

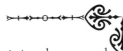

of mingled pleasure and guilt, as though without permission they grasped something belonging by right to others.

The bride dipped her hand into the well-trough, which was split at one end. At the other end where the water had collected, two or three bees were swimming, having fallen into the water in an attempt to drink. She stretched out her finger and the bees crawled in a single file along it to safety. They began to flutter their wings rapidly and rub them with their legs, their hind-legs swiftly wiping their bodies covered with fine hairs; they dragged their legs along her finger, leaving long tracks of moisture. Suddenly, one crawled higher and disappeared into her sleeve.

"It will sting you," the young man cried with a sudden movement.

But the girl stretched her arm downwards and shook the bee into the grass, her face glowing with pleasure at the man's concern.

Then both turned to listen to the dance music as the shrill notes of violins and bagpipes came from the bride's home. "They are searching for us," the girl whispered, and the young man nodded. They looked away from the lane, the house, the chimney which let out the smoke of festal cooking, and towards the plain before them, to which an early summer sun was setting in a cloudless sky. The purple rye fields formed an obtuse angle with the sky and behind them the west glowed with the promise of the coming harvest, as though it were written there in the heavens that the fields should give back their fruits tenfold. Behind the fence stretched the grazing ground, dear to them in its barrenness because of its promise of work for them. Further back the church stood erect—the only rising point on the plain—ruling the neighborhood, visible from every vantage point.

The summer air was alive with midges dancing everywhere. The bride sitting on the edge of the well felt them blindly strike against her face; she waved them away with a branch she had picked up, but even then they forced their way into her ears, her mouth, and her eyes. A sudden smarting in one eye, as though it had been stung, made her lift her hand to rub it.

"A midge flew into my eye," she said.

"Don't rub it—I'll take it out," the bridegroom answered hurriedly.

He had no need to bend down; standing opposite each other they were nearly the same height, eyes meeting. The man drew down the lid of her eye slightly, so that he could see the insect as a tiny black object on its inner surface. He brought his face still nearer, intending to remove it with his tongue, and in this position he saw what earlier had escaped him: the fine veins covering the white of her eye, the tiny freckles on her nose,

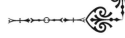

SHORT STORIES

spreading towards her cheeks. It was all beautiful to him and his thoughts turned towards his impending happiness. The girl knew, but continued to look openly at him with no hint of confusion, ready to surrender, yet without excitement, with calm, trusting eyes.

"Let's go in," she said, taking his hand in hers.

As they walked they became aware of a bent man approaching the lane from the highway. He moved slowly, dragging his steps. To the eyes of both he moved as one bidden to a funeral, not as a wedding guest.

"It is the oldest bailiff of the manor," the bridegroom remarked. "Do give him some ale."

The girl looked at him half in wonder, the same thought having just come to her that none but she should bring the welcoming tankard to this last guest.

She took a tankard with decorative carvings along its wooden sides and went into an adjoining building, but at the door she glanced instinctively back. The room seemed brighter to her than usual, and she could see that the faces of all who stood near the back window were drenched with the red glow of the sunset. Each time a couple danced past the window they swam for a time in a ruddy cloud. The new guest stood in the shadow.

The bride fumbled in the dark room for the tap of the barrel of ale when suddenly she started. The buzz of the rejoicing guests had suddenly altered its note—the entire house suddenly seemed to draw in its breath and sigh.... The bride's fingers clung uncertainly to the tankard, something heavy seemed to descend on her, a sudden desire to sit on the flour bin and weep— why, she could not have said, but she was afraid to return to the house.

With the foaming tankard in her hand she opened the door of the bridal room, stopping on the threshold so that ale dripped to the floor from the tankard. Her glance sped inquiringly around the room, but all eyes turned away before its question, seeking the floor. Only a vague sense of calamity remained, a hidden oppression seemed to bring the roof lower over their heads, the strings of the violins as mute as though they had suddenly stiffened. Many of the women began to weep, the men gazed darkly before them. She sought her mother with her eyes—the good woman's face was hidden by a shawl—her father—his eyes fixed to the floor—her husband...at last she caught a glance from him, but only for a moment, then his eyes avoided hers as well.

At the same time her father rose, suddenly having aged, his limbs hanging loosely as though crushed, as though bending before a great sorrow

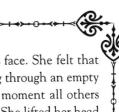

as he went toward an inner room, light fading from his face. She felt that she must follow him, but in going seemed to be walking through an empty chamber—she looked at no one, knowing that at this moment all others were but spectators, their curiosity and pity hurting her. She lifted her head so high up that her headgear almost swept the low ceiling. But as she passed her mother, she softened, her eyes begging her mother to follow; timidly, her mother rose, bathed in tears.

The door closed behind them.

"Say nothing," her mother said pleadingly to her father.

"How childish of mother to say that," the girl thought, instantly realizing that only love had dictated the words.

But she felt that the blow was coming....

"You are ordered to the manor for the night, my girl," her father said abruptly.

She opened her eyes—the blow had fallen. She was astounded to find herself still alive. A strong sense of resistance arose in her.

"You have sent me there, but I have not gone yet," she burst out sharply as though striking an invisible nail with a hammer.

"Here there is no mercy; such is the justice of the gentry," her father answered somberly.

She felt her father's words like weights on her proudly raised neck, forcing her to bow down. But she still resisted.

"Word is to be sent that no one comes from this house," she said.

Her father listened as to the speech of a child.

"How would it help us? They would drive us to the highway."

"Then we can beg, the whole lot of us."

"And you would be taken by force anyway."

She felt how the fetters around her were being drawn tighter, but still refused to yield.

"Let's go to the judge," she said.

"To meet the same gentry there. The Czar is high, God in his sky."

"Mother—and you?" she asked.

"You are neither the first nor the last, my child," her mother said between tears.

She looked helplessly at them, divining that neither intended to resist.

"Beg Jaan to come here," she said.

At the approach of the bridegroom she felt ashamed, as though guilty of some sin.

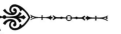

"Could you take me back—after that?" she whispered.

"I cannot say," the bridegroom replied. "I would take you back, but I don't know whether I should feel the same towards you," he added hurriedly by way of explanation.

"That's so—naturally," the bride humbly answered. "Though many others have gone and returned," she added, in a tone conveying that she only half believed her words.

"Others may go and come back, but one of your kind does not come back," the man replied, with added emphasis.

"Can you say what I should do?" she asked in agony.

"I myself don't know what to think yet," the man replied.

"It's not so much to me whether you take me back again, as whether you remain the same," the girl said, as if this thought had constantly occupied her and only now had found expression in words.

The girl looked at the man, but a mist seemed to divide them, and she was compelled to fumble for his hand as though she needed only to feel his presence. Suddenly it seemed that in the eyes looking at her through the mist something had sparkled—had he found a way out? she wondered. The hand tightly clenching her own was hot and trembling, as though the blood coursed fitfully through it. She felt a twitch and an unseen strength flow through it like a stream into her own veins. Something was born in the mist between them, something waxed—shapeless, terrifying.... The eyes seemed to ask something of her as they gazed at her in command, silently, wordlessly, they demanded something of her.... She tried to understand what he wanted, but the mist was before her, and she had to strain every faculty, was torn from herself and drawn up into those eyes... she began to tremble... the mist before her eyes turned red. Something indefinable united them at the moment, something, neither love nor hate, but a thought born simultaneously in them both.

Suddenly, the man bent forward, lips quivering, and she read on them a question:

"Do you dare?"

"I dare," she answered just as silently.

As though the mist had suddenly dissolved, they saw each other in a bright light, clear resolve in both pairs of eyes.

"But would you follow me to hard labor in Siberia?" the girl asked.

"I will follow wherever you are taken."

"But with what shall I...." the girl said, breaking off mid-sentence.

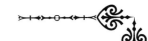

"With this," the man cautiously replied, drawing the knife from his belt.

They gazed coldly at each other, not as newly-weds, but as partners in crime in whom criminal doubt, even mutual anger, had taken root.

Suddenly the man melted.

"It's our wedding night," he exclaimed.

The girl was startled, but did not budge. And both understood that, not on a midsummer night such as this one, so bright and fragrant, would it come to them, but in the dark and foreboding gloom of a convict's hut in Siberia.

SHORT STORIES

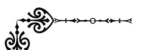

Getting Married

A. A. Milne

Probably you thought that getting married was quite a simple business. So did I. We were both wrong: it is the very dickens. Of course, I am not going to draw back now. As I keep telling Celia, her Ronald is a man of powerful fiber, and when he says he will do a thing, he does it—eventually. She shall have her wedding all right; I have sworn it. But I do wish that there weren't so many things to be arranged first.

The fact that we had to fix a day was broken to me one afternoon when Celia was showing me to some relatives of hers in the Addison Road. I got entangled with an elderly cousin on the hearth rug; and though I know nothing about motorcycles I talked about them for several hours under the impression that they were his subject. It turned out afterwards that he was equally ignorant of them, but thought they were mine. Perhaps we shall get on better at a second meeting. However, just when we were both thoroughly sick of each other, Celia broke off her gay chat with an aunt to say to me:

"By the way, Ronald, we did settle on the eleventh, didn't we?"

I looked at her blankly, my mind naturally full of motorcycles.

"The wedding," smiled Celia.

"Right-o," I said with enthusiasm. I was glad to be assured that I should not go on talking about motorcycles forever, and that on the eleventh, anyhow, there would be a short interruption for the ceremony. Feeling almost friendly to the cousin, I plunged into his favorite subject again.

On the way home Celia returned to the matter.

"Or would you rather it was the twelfth?" she asked.

"I've never heard a word about this before," I said. "It all comes as a surprise to me."

"Why, I'm *always* asking you."

"Well, it's very forward of you, and I don't know what young people are coming to nowadays. Celia, what's the *good* of my talking to your cousin for three hours about motorcycling? Surely one can get married just as well without that?"

"One can't get married without settling the day," said Celia, coming cleverly back to the point.

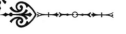

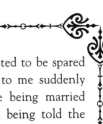

Well, I suppose one can't. But somehow I had expected to be spared the bother. I think my idea was that Celia would say to me suddenly one evening, "By the way, Ronald, don't forget we're being married to-morrow," and I should have said "Where?" And on being told the time and place I should have turned up pretty punctually; and after my best man had told me where to stand, and the clergyman had told me what to say, and my solicitor had told me where to sign my name, we should have driven from the church a happy married couple... and in the carriage Celia would have told me where we were spending the honeymoon.

However, it was not to be so.

"All right, the eleventh," I said. "Any particular month?"

"No," smiled Celia, "just any month. Or, if you like, every month."

"The eleventh of June," I surmised. "It is probably the one day in the year on which my uncle Thomas cannot come. But no matter. The eleventh let it be."

"Then that's settled. And at St. Miriam's?"

For some reason Celia has set her heart on St. Miriam's. Personally, I have no feeling about it. St. Andrew's-by-the-Wardrobe or St. Bartholomew's-Without would suit me equally well.

"All right," I said, "St. Miriam's."

There, you might suppose, the matter would have ended; but no.

"Then you will see about it to-morrow?" said Celia persuasively.

I was appalled at the idea.

"Surely," I said, "this is for you, or your father, or—or somebody to arrange."

"Of *course* it's for the bridegroom," protested Celia.

"In theory perhaps. But anyhow not the bridegroom personally. His best man... or his solicitor...or...I mean, you're not suggesting that I myself—. Oh, well, if you insist. Still, I must say I don't see what's the good of having a best man *and* a solicitor if—. Oh, all right, Celia, I'll go tomorrow.

So I went. For half an hour I padded round St. Miriam's nervously, and then summoning up all my courage, I knocked my pipe out and entered.

"I want," I said jauntily to a sexton or a sacristan or something—"I want—er—a wedding." And I added, "For two."

He didn't seem as nervous as I was. He inquired quite calmly when I wanted it.

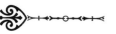

"The eleventh of June," I said. "It's probably the one day in the year on which my Uncle Thomas—. However, that wouldn't interest you. The point is that it's the eleventh."

The clerk consulted his wedding book. Then he made the surprising announcement that the only day he could offer me in June was the seventeenth. I was amazed.

"I am a very old customer," I said reproachfully. "I mean, I have often been to your church in my time. Surely—."

"We've weddings fixed on all the other days."

"Yes, yes, but you could persuade somebody to change his day, couldn't you? Or if he is very much set on being married on the eleventh you might recommend some other church to him. I dare say you know of some good ones. You see, Celia—my—that is, we're particularly keen for some reason on St. Miriam's."

The clerk didn't appreciate my suggestion. He insisted that the seventeenth was the only day.

"Then will you have the seventeenth?" he asked.

"My dear fellow, I can't possibly say off-hand," I protested. "I am not alone in this. I have a friend with me. I will go back and tell her what you say. She may decide to withdraw her offer altogether."

I went back and told Celia.

"Bother," she said. "What shall we do?"

"There are other churches. There's your own, for example."

"Yes, but you know I don't like that. Why *shouldn't* we be married on the seventeenth?"

"I don't know at all. It seems an excellent day; it lets in my Uncle Thomas. Of course, it may exclude my Uncle William, but one can't have everything."

"Then will you go and fix it for the seventeenth tomorrow?"

"Can't I send my solicitor this time?" I asked. "Of course, if you particularly want me to go myself, I will. But really, dear, I seem to be living at St. Miriam's nowadays."

And even that wasn't the end of the business. For, just as I was leaving her, Celia broke it to me that St. Miriam's was neither in her parish or in mine, and that, in order to qualify as a bridegroom, I should have to hire a room somewhere near.

"But I am very comfortable where I am," I assured her.

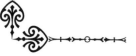

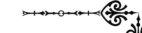

"You needn't live there, Ronald. You only want to leave a hat there, you know."

"Oh, very well," I sighed.

She came to the hall with me; and, having said good-bye to her, I repeated my lesson.

"The seventeenth, fix it up tomorrow, take a room near St. Miriam's, and leave a hat there. Good-bye."

"Good-bye.... And oh, Ronald!" She looked at me critically as I stood in the doorway. "You might leave *that* one," she said.

Short Stories

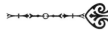

Selected Biographies

Bella Akhmadulina (b. 1937)

The daughter of Tartar and Italian parents, Akhmadulina was born in Moscow and attended the Gorky Institute of Literature (from which she was later expelled). She married poet Yevgeny Yevtushenko in her first marriage, then short story writer Yuri Nagibin, and finally an author of children's books, Gennadi Mamlin. Her first collection of poetry, *String*, was published in 1962, followed by *Music Lessons* in 1969.

Unnur Benediksdottir (b. 1881)

Writing under the pen-name "Hulda," she has born in Thingeyjarsysla in northeastern Iceland. She was raised there by her father, a librarian; her poetry reflects the influence of her homeland, especially her revival of *thulur*, or Icelandic rhapsodies, and her two-volume novel *Dalafólk* (1936 and 1939), a romantic description of life in rural Iceland. In addition, she has written sixteen books of poetry and numerous short stories, fairy tales, essays, and sketches.

Thomas Blacklock (1721–1791)

Also known as the "blind bard," Blacklock was born in Dumfriesshire, Scotland of English parents. Due to a severe case of small pox, he became completely blind when he was only six months old. His father, a bricklayer, died when Thomas was nineteen; he studied Latin, Greek, and French literature at Edinburgh University. He published his first volume of poetry in 1746, at the age of twenty-five.

Amy Bower (1881–)

Born in Tomales, California, she made her permanent residence in Santa Rosa. She was a regular contributor to several magazines and newspapers, including *Today's Humor*, *The New York Sun*, and the *Oakland Tribune*. She was a member of the League of Western Writers in Santa Rosa, California, where she made her home.

Anne Bradstreet (1612/1613–1672)

She was born in Northampton, England. After a difficult journey overseas, she and her husband Simon Bradstreet settled in Massachusetts. She

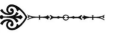

wrote *The Tenth Muse* (1650), a volume of poetry that was listed in William London's 1658 *Catalogue of the Most Vendible Books in England*, and that was well-received in London.

STEPHEN CRANE (1871–1900)

He was the son of the Reverend Dr. Jonathan Townley, born in Newark, New Jersey. His most famous novel, *Red Badge of Courage*, was published in 1895, when he 23 years old. His work was neglected until the 1920s when poets and writers such as Amy Lowell, Willa Cather, and Sherwood Anderson rediscovered him. Employed as a war correspondent, Crane traveled to Badenweiler, Germany, where he died of tuberculosis at the age of 28. In his lifetime, he was the author of six novels, over one hundred stories, and two books of poetry.

E. E. CUMMINGS (1894–1962)

Edward Estlin Cummings was born in Cambridge, Massachusetts. He was trained in Greek and Latin poetry (an influence felt later in his poetry), and majored in English at Harvard University. He published his first book of poetry, *The Enormous Room*, in 1922. Like many other American artists and writers, Cummings traveled to Paris in the 1920s only to be arrested and sent to a detention camp. Nevertheless, France did not lose its allure to him as he made frequent visits during the 1920s and 1930s. He died in Silver Lake, New Hampshire.

SAPARI DJOKO DAMONO (B. 1940)

The Indonesian poet was born in Solo, Central Java. His lyrical, yet disciplined and intellectual poetry has made him one of the most widely respected living Indonesian poets; he published his first collection of poetry, *The Eternal Sorrow of God*, in 1969.

FYODOR DOSTOEVSKY (1821–1881)

The creator of the modern psychological novel, Fyodor Mikhailovich Dostoevsky was born in Moscow, one of eight children, and from an early age suffered from epileptic fits. His father, a doctor of noble birth, was widowed when Fyodor was seventeen years old. He studied engineering in military school; while there, his father was murdered by serfs he had badly mistreated. His first novel, *Poor People* (1846), was well-received both by the public and by the famous critic Belinsky. He was arrested in 1849 as a

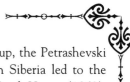

result of his membership to the Utopian socialist group, the Petrashevski Circle. His four years of experience at the prison in Siberia led to the largely autobiographical novel *Memoirs from the Dead House* (1862). Following the death of his older brother Mikhail, also a writer and an important influence on him, Fyodor lived abroad for six years. He published *Notes from Underground* in 1864, followed two years later by the publication of the seminal *Crime and Punishment*. He died of a hemorrhage in 1881.

JOHN ERSKINE (1879–1951)

Born in New York, New York, the educator, musician, and author was a professor of English at Columbia University; and between 1928 and 1937 he was president of the Julliard School of Music. An accomplished pianist, he published several books on music. He died of a heart attack in New York City.

ELIZABETH HEAD FETTER (1904–1973)

Also known as Hannah Lees, the pen-name she used in all her works, Fetter was born in Philadelphia, Pennsylvania, and received a B.A. from the University of Colorado in 1927. Her first published novel was *Women Will Be Doctors* (1939), and she was a regular contributor to numerous magazines, including *New Yorker, Saturday Evening Post,* and *Atlantic Monthly.* Between 1953 and 1956 she was a lecturer at Bryn Mawr College; she was also active in the social reform movement, joining such organizations as the National Association for the Advancement of Colored People and American Civil Liberties Union; she received the American Public Works Association Award in 1957.

JANOS GARAY (1812–1853)

The Hungarian poet, playwright, and journalist was born in Szekszárd. Popular in his time, he authored numerous long-forgotten heroic and epic poems while imitating Vörösmarty's ballad style. His most recognized poem, "The Discharged Soldier" (1943), provided Hungary with a national figure in its hero, Háry János.

JOHANN WOLFGANG VON GOETHE (1749–1832)

Indisputably the greatest writer of the German tradition, his life and work defines the Romantic period in Germany (late 18th Century to early 19th

Century), referred to as the Age of Goethe. His most influential works, *Sorrows of Werther* (1779) and *Faust, Parts One and Two* (1808 and 1931), continue to be read and studied. He died two months after making his final revisions of *Faust*.

ROBERT GRAVES (1895–1985)

The preeminent "minor" poet of the twentieth century, Graves was born in Wimbledon, London, and graduated from Oxford University in 1925. The recipient of numerous honors and prizes, Graves received the Hawthornden Prize for *I, Claudius* in 1935, the Gold Medal of the Poetry Society of America (1959), and was made an honorary member of the American Academy of Arts and Sciences in 1970. He died on the Spanish island of Majorca in the Mediterranean Sea.

JUDAH HALEVI (1085?–1140)

A physician by profession, Halevi was also a Spanish Hebrew poet and an Arabic philosopher. He lived in Granada, Toledo, and Cordova until finally settling in Palestine, Israel. He was the author of numerous works including *Kuzari*, a dialogue on Jewish religion and history written in Arabic, and *Songs of Zion*, a book of poetry. Weddings and friendship were common themes of his poetry.

GERARD MANLEY HOPKINS (1844–1889)

Born in Stratford, Essex, he is recognized as one of the greatest poets of the Victorian era. His mother, Kate Smith Hopkins, was a devout High Church Anglican, and his father, Manley Hopkins, was the founder of a marine insurance firm and an avid poet. Rediscovered after World War I, his style diverged from that of his contemporaries; he died in Dublin, Ireland of typhoid fever.

AINO KALLAS (1878–1956)

Publishing under the pseudonym Aino Suonio, Aino Julia Maria Kallas was born in Viipuri, Finland. The wife of an Estonian diplomat, most of her adult years were spent abroad, living in London between 1922 and 1934, in St. Petersburg from 1900 to 1903, and in Stockholm from 1944 to 1952. Yet, her works were written in seventeenth century archaic Finnish, and took as their primary theme Estonian peasant life. Among her most

notable works are the two-volume short story collection *From Beyond the Sea* (1904 and 1905), and *Päiväkirja*, five volumes of diary entries she had not intended for publication. She died in Helsinki.

VILHELM KRAG (1871–1933)

Vilhelm Andreas Wexels Krag was born in Kristiansand, Norway, and became established as the poet of Sorlandet. The novelist, poet, and playwright first received attention with the publication of his neo-Romantic poem "Fandango" (1891). He died in Sognafjord, an islet of the Norwegian Sea.

PÄR LAGERKVIST (1891–1974)

One of the most prolific, and also enigmatic, of Swedish literary figures, Lagerkvist was born in Växjö in the province of Småland, the youngest of seven children. First attracting notice with the publication of the poetry collection *Anguish* (1915), he authored several plays, including "The Last Man" (1917) and "The Difficult Hour" (1918), before turning to prose writing. Among his more well-known works are *The Dwarf* (1945), *Barabbas* (1950), *The Sibyl* (1958), and *The Death of Ahasuerus* (1962). He received the Nobel Prize for Literature in 1951; his acceptance speech was the first public speech he had ever given and, characteristically, his obligatory press conference merely drew from him the comment that he had no particular message to give. His son, Bengt Lagerkvist, is a well-known filmmaker.

SELMA LAGERLÖF (1858–1940)

Born in the southern province of Värmland, Selma Ottiliana Louis Lagerlöf moved to Stockholm in 1882 to attend the Women's Teachers College for Higher Education. The great success of her first novel, the classic epic tale *Gösta Berling's Saga*, in 1891, was followed by other successful works, and she resigned from her position as high school teacher in 1895 to devote herself to writing full-time. The two-volume geography book for children, *The Wonderful Adventures of Nils*, commissioned by the Swedish National Teacher's Society, was praised by Marguerite Yourcenar for its "wisdom and... poetry addressed to us all." She died of a stroke during the relief effort assisting the blockaded people of Finland on the estate she was born on.

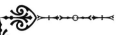

COMPTON MACKENZIE (1883–1972)

The son of two of the most successful actors of the late Victorian era (Edward Mackenzie and Virginia Bateman), Sir Edward Montague Compton Mackenzie lived a charmed life. His *Sinister Street* in two volumes (1913 and 1914), recounts the experiences of a young, upper-middle class boy, Michael Fane. Within his lifetime, Mackenzie produced over 100 books (almost half are novels).

A. A. MILNE (1882–1956)

Born in London and the son of a schoolmaster, Alan Alexander Milne attended Trinity College in Cambridge, where he received a mathematics degree in 1903. His first novel, *Lovers in London*, was published in 1905; the next year, he joined the editorial staff of the humor magazine *Punch*. His first play, *Wurzel-Flummery* (1917), was followed by the production, in New York and London, of over two dozen more in his lifetime. His most lasting contribution, however, is undoubtedly his four volumes of children's literature, particularly *The House at Pooh Corner* (1928). He died at his home in Sussex.

JOHN MILTON (1608–1674)

Best known for *Paradise Lost* (1674), Milton wrote polemical prose between the 1640s and 1650s while working as a foreign policy official. After years of dealing with steadily degrading eyesight, he went completely blind in 1652. He died in Artillery Walk near Bunhill Fields of complications from gout.

JAN BOLESLAW OZOG (B. 1913)

Born in Nienadówka, Poland, he graduated from the Theological Institute in Przemysl. As a result of the Nazi threat, Ozog joined the Home Army, an underground resistance movement, becoming an officer and later receiving the Gold Cross of Merit (1957) and the Medal of Victory and Freedom (1976).

BORIS PASTERNAK (1890–1960)

The 1958 Nobel Prize Winner was born in Moscow, where he later attended the University. During the First World War, he was rejected for service due to health reasons; after the 1917 revolution, he was employed at the People's Commissariat for Education. In 1922 he published *My Sister, Life*, a volume of poetry praised by Marina Tsvetaeva, a poet who

would become a close friend and critical influence on his work. From the 1930s until the foreign release of *Dr. Zhivago* (which was banned in the Soviet Union), he did not release any works other than translations, most notably of Shakespeare. In 1960 he died from cancer of the lungs.

EDGAR ALLAN POE (1809–1849)
The son of actors, Poe was born in Boston, Massachusetts; his father deserted his family and his mother died when he was two years old. He moved to Richmond, Virginia, where John Allan, a merchant, took care of him until he returned to Boston alone in 1827. Poe spent two years in the army, and in 1836 married his fourteen-year-old cousin. His last years were spent earning a meager income as a journalist and editor. He gained popularity with "The Raven" (1845) and his short story, "The Gold Bug" (1843). He died in Baltimore, Maryland, after being found unconscious in a polling booth.

W. S. RENDRA (B. 1935)
The "Tom Jones of Indonesian Poetry" was born in Solo, central Java, and is regarded as the foremost living Indonesian poet. He is variously termed a nature poet, imagist, and balladic narrator. His mother is a dancer of the traditional Javanese *serimpi*, and his father is the teacher of Indonesian and Old Javanese. His attentions are primarily directed at the theater, for which he writes, acts, translates, and directs.

CHRISTINA ROSSETTI (1830–1894)
Born in London (and later ending her life there), Rossetti's *Goblin Market and Other Poems* (1862) marked the first literary success of the Pre-Raphaelites. She was called by Ford Maddox Ford the "greatest master of words… that the nineteenth century gave us." She died of cancer in 1894, still a devout member of the Anglican Sisterhood.

GEORGE SARANDARIS (1907–1941)
He was born in Constantinople but moved to Italy at the age of two, staying there until he was twenty-four. He received a law degree in Macerata; he never practiced law, instead translating Italian and Greek poetry. He published four volumes of poetry, a book of prose poems, and three books of philosophy. Sarandaris went to Greece in 1931 to serve in the military and died from hardships suffered as a common soldier in the Albanian War.

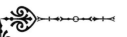

SENRYŪ POETRY (LATE 18TH CENTURY-EARLY 19TH CENTURY JAPAN)

Reaching its peak in late eighteenth century Edo, its name was taken from Karai Senryū (1718–1790), a leading *tenja* (marker) from Edo. Using submissions, he compiled the best verses in *Yanagidaru* collections, totaling twenty-four by 1791. With identical form as haiku, senryū's distinction lies primarily in subject matter; while haiku poetry deals with nature, senryū deals with people. In addition, the language used is common, and was considered more entertainment than poetry. Following the Kansei reforms, senryū lost its original spirit, and is used by few poets today.

SHIN SHALOM (B. 1904)

The poet, short story writer, playwright, and literary critic, was educated in Germany and moved to Palestine in 1922. His more important works were symbolist poems, as well as translations of Shakespeare's sonnets. His collected works were published in 1971 and fill seven volumes.

EDITH SODERGRAN (1892–1923)

Educated at a German school at the then-Leningrad, Edith Irene Sodergran's first volume of poetry, *Dikter* (1916), evinces her expressionistic style. The Finnish-Swedish poet and author developed consumption at age 16, a condition that eventually killed her. As a result of the Russian Revolution, she was forced to move and spend the last five years of her life in poverty.

KIM SOWOL (1902–1934)

Two volumes of poetry by Sowol have been published, *Azaleas* in 1925, and *Selected Poems* posthumously in 1939. She died at the age of 32.

STATIUS (A.D. 45–A.D. 96)

Publius Papinius Statius wrote several epic poems, including *Thebaid* (A.D. 91), but it was his short poems that received attention. His short poems comprise five books.

EVERT TAUBE (1890–1976)

Bon in Göteborg, Sweden, Taube was a poet, prose writer, and modern troubadour who wrote, composed, and sung his own songs. A selection of his songs, *Hjärtats nyckel heter sång*, were published in 1960. He is also the

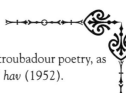

author of *Vallfart* (1957), a novel about Provence and troubadour poetry, as well as the autobiographical *Jagkommer av ett brusand' hav* (1952).

BAYARD TAYLOR (1825–1878)

Known as the "Great American Traveler" (a title he despised), Taylor was born in Kennett Square, Pennsylvania, to parents of English-German ancestry and Quaker leanings. His first poem was published in the *Saturday Evening Post* when he was sixteen. His numerous walking tours, commissioned by various publishers, resulted in a long list of poetry books. He died in Germany after accepting an appointment as Minister to Germany.

SAUL TCHERNIKHOVSKY (1873–1943)

A trained doctor, Tchernikhovsky practiced medicine in Russia before moving to Palestine in 1931. Nicknamed "the Heathen," the author of love lyrics and pantheistic songs, he was also a translator, most notably of *Gilgamesh, Iliad,* and *Odyssey,* with all translations metrically true.

DYLAN THOMAS (1914–1953)

Born in Swansea, Wales in a middle-class family, Thomas' life and work have spawned lasting controversy. The poet was also the author of short stories such as *Portrait of the Artist as a Young Dog* (1940) and *A Child's Christmas in Wales* (1955). He was married to Caitlin Macnamara, a relationship which was intense as the rest of his life; on his fourth and final American tour, he died at Saint Vincent's Hospital in New York, New York, as a result of years of heavy drinking. He is buried in Laugharne where a simple white cross marks his grave.

WILLIAM THOMAS WALSH (1891–1949)

He was born in Waterbury, Connecticut, and graduated from Yale University in 1913, later receiving an honorary degree from Fordham (1933). A teacher, reporter, biographer, and poet, he is the author of *Life of St. Teresa of Avila* (1942). He was granted the highest cultural honor by Spain in a double ceremony in 1944, receiving both the Cross of Comendador of the Civil Order of Alfonso the Wise and the Catholic Literary Award of the Gallery of Living Catholic Authors.

YVOR WINTERS (1900–1968)

The poet was born in Chicago, Illinois, but grew up in Eagle Rock,

California; in 1918, he discovered that he had tuberculosis and was sent to a sanitarium in Santa Fe, New Mexico until 1922. Influenced by the Japanese poetry and Native American songs he studied while in the sanitarium, he wrote *The Immobile Wind* (1921) and *The Magpie's Shadow* (1922). Following the publication of his best work, *Collected Poems* (1952), he won the Bollington Prize for Poetry (1961). His daughter, Janet Lewis, became an accomplished poet and author.

Wedding Books from Hippocrene . . .

"I DO, I DO": AMERICAN WEDDING ETIQUETTE OF YESTERYEAR

If there is any occasion for which good manners are a must, it is a wedding! With excerpts from ten authorities on wedding etiquette, including Emma Albert Cole, Ann Page, and Emily Post, this wonderfully unique book remembers American wedding customs from the colonial days to the 1920s. Discover the surprising origins of the terms "honeymoon" and "best man," peek inside the 19th century bride's trousseau, and follow couples through traditions and customs that may seem quirky and amusing, as well as moving and sentimental, by today's standards.

120 pages • 6 x 9 • 0-7818-0650-X • W • $17.50hc • (730)

POLISH WEDDING CUSTOMS AND TRADITIONS

Sophie Hodorowicz Knab

From bestselling author, Sophie Hodorowicz Knab, comes this unique planning guide for Americans who want to organize and celebrate a Polish-style wedding. Sections titled Engagement, Bridal Flowers, Wedding Clothes, Ceremony, Reception and even Baby Names, will assist the bride-and groom-to-be through every step of the wedding process. Special tips on "How to Draw from the Past" at the end of each chapter provide helpful suggestions on how to incorporate Polish tradition into the modern wedding, to make it a truly distinctive and unforgettable event. Photographs and illustrations throughout.

Sophie Hodorowicz Knab is author of *Polish Herbs, Flowers & Folk Medicine* and *Polish Customs, Traditions & Folklore*. She writes a column for the *Polish American Journal* and resides in Grand Island, N.Y.

196 pages • 6 x 9 • photos/illustrations • 0-7818-0530-9 • W • $19.95hc • (641)

UNDER THE WEDDING CANOPY: LOVE AND MARRIAGE IN JUDAISM

David C. and Esther R. Gross

This comprehensive book delves into the wide range of marriage customs, ceremonies, traditions and practices that have become part of the Jewish heritage for nearly four thousand years.

"An ideal gift for couples . . . practical, full of useful information."
—*The Forward*

"Jewish wedding customs from around the world . . . advice on how to create a happy marriage." —*American Jewish World*

"A portrait of Jewish marriage that is unfailingly positive and unabashedly traditional." —*Na'amat*

243 pages • 5 ½ x 8 ¼ • 0-7818-0481-7 • W • $22.50hc • (596)

Love Poetry from Hippocrene . . .

CLASSIC AMERICAN LOVE POEMS

These verses of love express a unique American voice on the subject. This lovely anthology comes in a charmingly illustrated gift edition, with nearly 100 poems of love from 50 American poets, including Anne Bradstreet, Edna St. Vincent Millay, James Wright and Robert Lowell.

130 pages • 6 x9 • illustrations • 0-7818-0645-3 • $17.50hc • (731) • May

CLASSIC ENGLISH LOVE POEMS

edited by Emile Capouya

This lovely anthology comes in a charming gift edition and contains 95 classic poems of love from 45 poets that have continued to inspire over the years. Beautifully illustrated throughout.

130 pages • 6 x 9 • illustrations • 0-7818-0572-4 • $17.50hc • (671)

CLASSIC FRENCH LOVE POEMS

edited by Lisa Neal

This lovely gift edition contains 77 inspiring love poems translated into English from French, the language of love itself, including a complete translation of Paul Géraldy's *Toi et Moi*. Also featured are 25 beautiful illustrations from famous artist Maurice Leloir.

130 pages • 6 x 9 • illustrations • 0-7818-0573-2 • W • $17.50hc • (672)

SCOTTISH LOVE POEMS: A PERSONAL ANTHOLOGY, RE-ISSUED EDITION

edited by Lady Antonia Fraser

Lady Fraser collects the loves and passions of her fellow Scots, from Burns to Aileen Campbell Nye, into a book that will find a way to touch everyone's heart.

253 pages • 5 1/2 x 8 1/4 • 0-7818-0406-X • NA • $14.95pb • (482)

HEBREW LOVE POEMS

edited by David C. Gross

illus. by Shraga Weil

Several translators have reworked over 90 love lyrics from biblical times to current poetry written in modern Israel.

"A volume of great beauty and range." —*Booklist*

91 pages • 6 x 9 • illus. • 0-7818-0430-2 • $14.95pb • (473)

IRISH LOVE POEMS: DÁNTA GRÁ
edited by Paula Redes
illus. by Peadar McDaid
Mingling the famous, the infamous, and the unknown into a striking collection, these works span four centuries up to the most modern of poets such as Nuala Ni Dhomhnaill and Brendan Kennelly.
146 pages • 6 x 9 • illus. • 0-7818-0396-9 • W • $17.50hc • (70)

Love Quotations and Proverbs

TREASURY OF LOVE QUOTATIONS FROM MANY LANDS
This charming gift volume contains over 500 quotations from 400 great writers, thinkers and personalities—all on the subject of love. These are words of wit and wisdom from all over the world (over 40 countries and languages), from antiquity to present day. With lovely illustrations throughout, this volume is the perfect gift of love for anyone.
144 pages • 6 x 9 • illustrations • 0-7818-0574-0 • W • $17.50hc   (673)

TREASURY OF LOVE PROVERBS FROM MANY LANDS
This anthology includes more than 600 proverbs on love from over 50 languages and cultures, addressing such timeless experiences as first love, unrequited love, jealousy, marriage, flirtation and attraction. Charming illustrations throughout.
146 pages • 6 x 9 • illustrations • 0-7818-0563-5 • W • $17.50hc • (698)

All prices subject to change. To purchase Hippocrene Books contact your local bookstore, call (718) 454-2366, or write to: HIPPOCRENE BOOKS, 171 Madison Avenue, New York, NY 10016. Please enclose check or money order, adding $5.00 shipping (UPS) for the first book and $.50 for each additional book.